FOR BREW FREAKS, BEAN GEEKS, AND THE SIMPLY CURIOUS ...

Fig.1 Coffea Arabica

HELPING TO GROW
THE SPECIALITY COFFEE CULTURE

SOUTH WEST AND SOUTH WALES INDEPENDENT COFFEE GUIDE

the INSIDER'S GUIDE TO SPECIALITY COFFEE VENUES AND ROASTERS

★ ★ ★ ★ ★ ★ ★ ★ ★ ★ ★

Nº 3

Salt Media, 5 Cross Street, Devon, EX31 1BA.
www.saltmedia.co.uk
Tel: 01271 859299
Email: ideas@saltmedia.co.uk

Salt Media *Independent Coffee Guide* team:
Nick Cooper, Kathryn Lewis, Lisa McNeil, Tamsin Powell,
Jo Rees, Rosanna Rothery, Emma Scott-Goldstone,
Chris Sheppard, Dale Stiling, Katie Taylor and Mark Tibbles.
Design and illustration: Salt Media

**A big thank you to the *Independent Coffee Guide*
committee** (meet them on page 180) for their expertise
and enthusiasm, **our headline sponsors** Schluter,
Yeo Valley and Cimbali, **and sponsors** Beyond the Bean,
Bunn, Cakesmiths, Clifton Coffee Roasters,
Extract Coffee Roasters, Roastworks Coffee Co.
and SCAE.

Coffee shops, cafes and roasters are invited to be
included in the guide based on meeting criteria set by
our committee, which includes a high quality coffee
experience for visitors, use of speciality beans and
being independently run.

For information on the South West and South Wales,
Northern and Scottish *Independent Coffee Guides*, visit:
www.indycoffee.guide

🐦 @indycoffeeguide
📷 @indycoffeeguide

Chow Down

HUB ST IVES

№ 72

9 CRAFT BEERS ON OUR TAPS!

ORIGIN COFFEE

HELSTON 16 MILES

As the coffee scene takes another great leap forward, it's my pleasure to introduce our third edition.

It's significantly bigger – and better, of course – this year, and packed with even more must-visits across the South West and, for the first time, South Wales.

It's been a hugely enjoyable journey putting this guide together – from tracking down roasters in the wilds of west Wales to discovering a little slice of Melbourne in Ilfracombe, north Devon.

Those coffee tours are a joy, even if it sometimes means enduring the gut-churning effect of too much caffeine at the end of a long day visiting cafes and roasteries.

To make *your* adventuring easier, we've introduced a new fold-out map in this edition, as well as bringing more establishments into the guide which meet the criteria, so you'll find somewhere good to go, wherever you are.

New coffee shops and roasteries are springing up each week, so follow us on social media to stay up to date with new finds. We've also introduced a monthly coffee guide enewsletter and competitions. Sign up to join in at www.indycoffee.guide and never have a bad coffee again.

Jo Rees
Indy Coffee Guides editor

'THE GUT-CHURNING, EFFECT OF TOO MUCH CAFFEINE AT THE END OF A COFFEE TOUR'

CONTENTS

12 WELCOME
14 MAN VS MACHINE
18 STILL LIFE IN THE OLD BEAN?
22 BEAN QUEENS
26 COFFEE ON TAP
30 THE POD SQUAD
34 YOUR JOURNEY STARTS HERE

36 CAFES
38 SOUTH WALES
50 GLOUCESTERSHIRE
58 BRISTOL, BATH & SOMERSET
90 WILTSHIRE & DORSET
102 DEVON
116 CORNWALL
124 MORE GOOD CUPS

131 ROASTERS
156 MORE GOOD ROASTERS

158 COFFEE GLOSSARY
162 INDEX
168 MAPS
169 CARDIFF MAP
170 BRISTOL MAP
172 BATH MAP
173 EXETER MAP
178 SOUTH WEST & SOUTH WALES MAP
180 MEET OUR COMMITTEE

f three is the magic number, it stands to reason that this, the third edition of the *South West Independent Coffee Guide*, is a special one.

The South West is where our journey began, but this year has been a rollercoaster ride with the second edition of the Northern guide and the first ever Scottish guide launched. A huge thanks goes to our sponsors who've helped make this happen.

In No. 3, we're excited to welcome South Wales. With so many great independent and high quality cafes and roasteries just across the bridge, we couldn't leave them out any longer. If you haven't yet checked out the coffee scene in South Wales, you're missing out on some of the UK's very best coffee experiences.

As a committee, our job is to maintain the integrity of the guide. With a focus on the independence of all the businesses featured, as well as the roasting and service of speciality grade coffees, this year's book is even bigger than the last – evidence of the growth in the sector within our region.

Speciality coffee is one of the most dynamic industries in the country right now, and each year we see many advances in quality, equipment, style and knowledge. There's never been a better time to be in the coffee world and our goal

'THE GUIDE'S HERE TO HELP YOU DISCOVER SOME SPECIAL FINDS'

is to help lure consumers out of the big chains and into the independent cafes.

To help you take the experience further, we've developed the website and plan to launch an interactive app. And you can even get your hands on a limited edition *Indy Coffee Guide* mug online now.

Enjoy drinking your way around the South West and South Wales. Here's to another great year of great coffee.

Andrew Tucker
Founding guide member and head of coffee at Clifton Coffee Roasters

We challenged Robert Ward of Cimbali – which manufactures both traditional and super automatic coffee machines – to referee the man vs machine debate and consider if technology could deal the ultimate blow to the barista?

BUMP AND GRIND

The coffee grinder plays a crucial role in a great cup of coffee, but do the new super automatic machines, with their inbuilt grinding systems, work as well as a separate grinder operated by the barista?

BARISTA

Most artisan cafes use grind-on-demand grinders, which work on a timer so optimum dosing can be achieved. It makes them pretty accurate, helping the barista to consistently pull decent shots.

BEAN-TO-CUP

Next generation coffee machines like Cimbali's S30 are fitted with induction motors and prove to be just as accurate.

VERDICT

'I feel a draw is in order on this one,' says Robert. 'The only way to improve consistency would be to have scales on the portafilter – but the benefits would be negligible.'

HOLD THE PRESS

Correct tamping ensures an even flow of water through the coffee, which is essential to extract the fullest flavour from the grounds. Yet who comes out on top when it comes to tamping?

BARISTA

In a busy service, uneven manual tamping can be an issue, leading to the possibility of channelling (gaps through which the water flows more quickly) causing under-extraction.

BEAN-TO-CUP

A good bean-to-cup won't tamp unevenly, or at a different pressure or compaction.

VERDICT

'I think this one might just go to the machine, although it's worth mentioning the development of the Push Tamp by Clockwork Espresso, which, when set correctly, can give the mechanical consistency of a bean-to-cup machine.'

Beyond the Bean Ltd.
Independently owned and run since 1997

Proud sponsor of the South West Coffee Guide
+44 (0)117 953 3522 // @beyondthebean

ROUND 3
SIZING UP THE COMPETITION

When it comes to shot volume, what works best? Volumetrics, gravimetrics, manual scales and a stop button, or just the skilled eye of a barista? Cimbali pitted two of its team against each other to find out.

BARISTA

Tim Medley, who has worked for a number of years in speciality coffee, used scales, his eye and whatever else he could find. A good consistency was achieved by using volumetrics with only a 1-2g maximum variance.

BEAN-TO-CUP

Rohan Pitumpe, runner up UK Latte Art Champion, pressed the button on a bean-to-cup machine and a decent consistency was achieved via volumetrics.

VERDICT

'It seems using technology on both types of machine is a real advantage in terms of consistency,' says Robert. 'Although a couple of times when making multiple drinks and using milk, shots that weren't stopped automatically led to wasted or inconsistent shots.'

ROUND 4
CRUNCH TIME

When it comes to achieving the perfect shot time, who clocks in with the most consistency, the barista or the high-performance machine?

BARISTA

If we use time as a control point (as a lot of cafes do), it means monitoring every shot and making micrometric adjustments to grinders as temperature, humidity, degassing and other variables change. Machines that display shot times help with consistency.

BEAN-TO-CUP

Machines like the S30 and M100 GT, with their Perfect Grind Systems, monitor every shot produced. When the average shot time starts to drift, they make small adjustments to both grind time for dose consistency and grind size for shot flow consistency.

VERDICT

'If we use technology on both then this is a draw – as long as the barista is consistent. So maybe the bean-to-cup just pips it.'

CONCLUSION

'The main thing is not to be afraid of the developments but to embrace the elements of technology that benefit the coffee industry. Technical baristas will always be needed to set recipes, taste the coffee and make adjustments as needed. Service baristas will be the ones who really engage with customers and help grow the business, maintaining that essential personal interaction,' says Rob.

STILL LIFE IN THE OLD BEAN?

For food bursting with flavour, most would agree that fresh seasonal eating is the way to go. But does the same apply to coffee? Can beans actually improve with age or should we all be insisting on fresh-crop coffee with our croissant? We asked the opinion of green bean importer, Phil Schluter

RAIN CHECK

The bountiful beans that we roast, grind and brew are the seeds of fruit and, just like tomatoes or oranges, there is an ultimate time to pick them. Coffee cherries mature in the months following flowering, triggered by a growing region's rainy season.

In most east African countries, explains Phil, there are two distinct rainy seasons. The main rains, which are longer and heavier, giving the main coffee crop. And shorter, light rains which lead to a smaller fly crop. But the main crop doesn't necessarily always yield the best-tasting coffee.

'There is more coffee to choose from with the main crop, but in Kenya, for example, the highest grown co-op coffees from the main crop will arrive at the same time as the fly crop of the lowest-grown estates,' says Phil.

'Maturation is sufficiently slower on the highest ground so the two crops run into each other. Therefore, I always encourage buyers to base decisions purely on cup quality, not on time of year or whether a coffee is from the main or fly crop. Each needs to be judged on its merits and inherent flavours.'

TOP-OF-THE-CROPS

"The fresher the bean, the better the flavour" goes the mantra. Yet, given the variations in harvest conditions and the ability of new packaging to keep coffee fresh, Phil believes "fresh crop" isn't necessarily a shorthand for "quality".

'There's a false assumption that only new crop coffee tastes good and is worth buying,' he says. *'But if roasters are willing to cup blind, so they are not prejudiced about what a coffee should taste like they'll sometimes surprise themselves. A coffee which has been in Europe for eight or nine months, which is no longer seen as fresh crop, can cup really well and is frequently less expensive than the new crop coffee.'*

'THERE'S A FALSE ASSUMPTION THAT ONLY NEW CROP COFFEE TASTES GOOD'

NO COUNTRY FOR OLD COFFEE

Does it all go downhill for the aging coffee bean? According to Phil, two things happen to coffee as time goes by.

'The first is that it picks up a woody or straw-like flavour,' he says. *'At best this can taste similar to a pleasant tobacco-like finish. At worst it tastes like old earthy wood. The colour of the beans will also gradually fade.'*

While some caffeine fans like the taste of a woody aged cup, the coffee connoisseur will want to avoid "past-crop" flavour.

'The second thing which can happen is that the coffee can pick up a baggy, jute or petrol taint. This is unpleasant, but it's much less common in coffee which is shipped in Grain Pro or Ecotact liners.'

How quickly a coffee ages will depend more than anything else on its initial drying process and the altitude at which it's grown.

'HOW QUICKLY A COFFEE AGES WILL DEPEND MORE THAN ANYTHING ELSE ON ITS INITIAL DRYING PROCESS AND THE ALTITUDE AT WHICH IT'S GROWN'

'Higher grown, harder beans age more slowly,' explains Phil. *'Lower grown, softer beans age faster. If the initial drying of the parchment for washed coffee is not done to 11 or 12 per cent humidity, the bean will not seal itself well. Even if the coffee is later dried to the correct level, it will fade faster (become white, yellow and bleached) and will start tasting woody more quickly.'*

NOT EASY BEING GREEN

While many foods burst with flavour when fresh some, like great wine and cheese, require patience to be at their optimum.

Coffee, once it has been harvested, needs to rest in parchment to be at its prime. For the speciality industry, immaturity can be as much a problem as age.

'If you cup new crop Tanzania coffees in late July, they will taste a little green, fresh and unripe,' says Phil. *'However, you need to be able to see past that to detect the flavours which will develop as that green flavour fades. Roasters who wait until a coffee sample cups perfectly, might find that the best coffee has already sold out.'*

SMALL IS BEAUTIFUL

Peak season beans may pack a punch, yet that's not the only factor affecting the flavour of your favourite brew, according to Phil.

'Coffee is a seasonal product and as with all agricultural products, each crop is different,' he says. *'Weather and care in processing make the biggest impact on the variation in flavour each year. As with wine, drier weather and a smaller harvest tend to yield better flavours. As a rule of thumb, we say that there is the same total flavour in each crop – so if the crop is smaller, there is more flavour concentrated in each bean.'*

ARABICA

HARVEST MONTHS ACROSS THE GLOBE

CENTRAL AMERICA

EL SALVADOR, GUATEMALA, HONDURAS, MEXICO, NICARAGUA
Nov-Feb/Mar

AFRICA

ETHIOPIA Sep-Jan
BURUNDI/RWANDA Mar-Jul
KENYA/DRC/UGANDA Oct-Aug*
*2 crops a year
TANZANIA/ZIMBABWE/ZAMBIA Jul-Dec

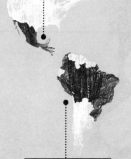

ASIA

INDIA Dec-Mar
INDONESIA Jun-Dec
PAPUA NEW GUINEA Apr-Aug

SOUTH AMERICA

BRAZIL May-Sep

COLOMBIA Sep-Mar*
*second small crop

PERU May-Nov

BOLIVIA Jun-Oct

'IF THE CROP IS SMALLER, MORE FLAVOUR IS CONCENTRATED IN EACH BEAN'

BEAN QUEENS

SISTERS DOING IT FOR THEMSELVES

A hot topic at Re:co's Coffee Symposium in Dublin was the role of women in coffee. We asked trainer, consultant and owner of Coffea Arabica, Daisy Rollo, about some of the remarkable women who have inspired her own love affair with the bean

Clockwise from left: **Women singing while sorting coffee at a Konga Washing Station in Ethiopia; Daisy Rollo running a latte art course at Leaze Farm coffee school; a woman sorting coffee to export at Moplaco in Ethiopia; Heleanna Georgalis preparing a cupping table in Addis Ababa.**

The mesmeric cadence of women's voices rising and falling as they gather colourful cherries in the sunshine is one of many inspiring and enduring memories Daisy Rollo carries with her from her research trips to plantations across the globe.

'It's not unusual to listen to a woman serenading herself while picking, or a group of women singing together as they sort the coffee,' says Daisy who has visited Costa Rica, India, Ethiopia, Panama, Vietnam and Cuba in her quest to learn all that she can about growing and cultivating coffee.

'It's really stunning! They always look so proud, are always smiling and there is a great community spirit. It's good to know the journey of the bean starts with such dedication and passion. If I was asked to name some unsung female heroes of coffee I would have to start with these women.'

Daisy, who has made short documentaries about the farms she's visited, has witnessed women working in all areas of speciality coffee at source, from neutering the plant through to picking, processing, sorting and exporting.

'One of the highlights of my career is to see people working hard to deliver the best and being paid a fair price for it; to be proud of a product that is recognised all over the world.'

TRAILBLAZER

In Ethiopia, Daisy stayed three weeks with Heleanna Georgalis, the daughter of Yanni Georgalis, founder of Moplaco, one of the oldest quality exporters in Addis Ababa.

After the sudden death of her father in 2008, Heleanna was faced with a difficult decision: to continue the legacy her father had painstakingly built or to follow the path she had created for herself.

EXTRACTCOFFEE.CO.UK

EXTRACT COFFEE ROASTERS

Roasted on → BIG BERTHA, VINTAGE BETTY, BARRY & JAMES OUR HAND RESTORED DRUM ROASTERS

FRESHLY ROASTED & POSTED FROM BRISTOL

FREE SHIPPING ON ALL COFFEE

EXTRACTCOFFEE.CO.UK

Despite a limited knowledge of the coffee business she immersed herself in learning about roasting, cupping, agronomy and niche speciality coffee markets.

'Heleana is an inspiration to me. The labour of love she is putting into Moplaco is incredible. After the death of her dad, she took on the responsibility of running the company and continues to do it with the same love, passion and quality as her father.

'A lot of work is involved in travelling the country, visiting plantations, processing, receiving clients, assessing coffee quality, selling at auctions ... the list goes on. Her dedication to quality is next to none.'

PERSONALITY AND PASSION

Today, in her role as an independent trainer, Daisy finds herself inspired by the many women working across the industry as baristas, trainers, importers, exporters and professional cuppers. The opportunities for women in coffee are endless.

'At Leaze Farm coffee school in Bristol or at The London School Of Coffee where I teach, there are equal numbers of women and men turning up for courses, all keen to understand how to produce the best cup of coffee, its origins and how to taste it.

'Coffee is a vast world, but once you have the opportunity to sample great quality cups, a seed is planted. There are opportunities for everyone to learn more, to expand their knowledge and work in the industry.

'The beauty is that there are so many diverse directions you can take on a path that is only just starting to be built by both men and women.'

Daisy doesn't necessarily think women play a separate or different role to men in the industry.

'I think both genders bring something to the table in their own way. It's all about personality and passion,' she says.

'COFFEE IS A VAST WORLD, BUT ONCE YOU HAVE THE OPPORTUNITY TO SAMPLE GREAT QUALITY CUPS, A SEED IS PLANTED'

COFFEE
ON
TAP

The brewing trend that's making waves across the pond, nitro has turned up at a select handful of British festivals, bars and cafes this year. Not tried it? Let us introduce you to the smooth stuff

NITRO-DUCTIONS

Slow brewed in cold water overnight then propelled into a tall glass in a foamy infusion of nitrogen, this wonderfully geeky serve style is the latest way to meet your speciality caffeine fix. We got the low-down from a few insiders well acquainted with the new brew on the block ...

THE GEEKY BIT

'The whole concept of nitro cold brew takes a lot from the brewing industry,' explains Ben Barker of Yorkshire's Artemis Cold Brew, one of the brew buffs pushing nitro at festivals and events up and down the UK. *'We've adopted the methods that brewers use to produce the smoother mouthfeel of a stout or porter, to create the creamy texture akin to Guinness in a chilled coffee drink.'*

Combining single origin cold brew with nitrogen gas, the wickedly smooth yield is achieved when the coffee is released from a chilled keg through a pressurised tap. *'In coffee, this method is used as much for the aesthetic appeal as it is for the texture and taste,'* adds Ben.

THE TASTY BIT

'The gas itself has no flavour,' continues Ben, *'but it changes the concept of the drink completely. The smooth texture from the nitro allows us to bridge the gap between black coffee and milk, as the resulting creaminess changes the delicate flavours of the coffee. For example dark chocolate notes will become milk chocolate. It's a great way to get people who aren't fans of black coffee to make the transition into cold brew.'*

'A CREAMY TEXTURE AKIN TO GUINNESS IN A CHILLED COFFEE DRINK'

Calling all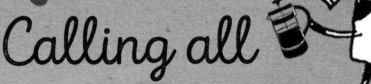

COFFEE
LOVERS

...show your milk the
♥ you show your beans!

Buy British milk to reduce
the food miles in your cup

Our cows are fed on an organic
diet, free from pesticides + GMOs

Our farmers are guaranteed
a fair price for their milk

So you can rest assured
you're getting great
taste the right way!

Yeo Valley Organic Whole Milk

yeo
valley
FAMILY FARM

Find out more at:
yeovalley.co.uk/milklovers

So can we blast any bean with gas for a refreshingly foamy mouthfeel? Well, no, as Don Iszatt of Finca in Dorchester, one of the few South West speciality shops serving nitro, explains. *'When we prepare the cold brew for our nitro offering, we always start by selecting the right single origin for the job. Fruity, citrus and floral tones don't usually work well with the creamier and sweeter yield of the infusion. We'd normally choose coffees with nuttier, chocolatey characteristics.'*

THE HOW-DO-I-GET-MY-HANDS-ON-IT? BIT

Nitro went mainstream in America a couple of years ago, with New York's Stumptown Coffee Roasters leading the way with nitro on draft in its stores and even a canned version for the retail market. *'The UK is a little late to the nitro party,'* says Ben, *'but at Artemis we've been doing this for almost two years and people are starting to catch on to the trend.'*

The slow take-up of the silky brew at speciality shops could be due to the perceived intricacies of the set-up, as Don explains, *'There are a number of things cafes have to consider when setting up nitro, including how they'll brew the cold coffee, storage, bottling, kegging and shelf life.'*

But it's easier than they may think, as Ben butts in: *'coffee shop owners seem to think nitro will take up lots of space, but our set-up requires less than a metre squared. We also offer kegs of speciality cold brew with a lengthy shelf life.'*

THE ALTERNATIVE TO BEER BIT

So are we all going to be swapping pints for cold brew? Well, maybe. *'Bars and shops with a line-system already in place for craft beer could be serving cold brew right now,'* enthuses Ben. *'And the micro-foam is great for cocktails – we're already working on a speciality espresso martini on-tap.'*

We'll raise a glass to that.

THE
POD
SQUAD

Speciality coffee fans have traditionally been a bit sniffy about coffee capsules of the Nespresso type, however with coffee guru Maxwell Colonna-Dashwood, and Will Little of Devon's Roastworks Coffee Co., embracing the technology for speciality beans, that may be about to change

Speciality beans represent just 6% of the global coffee harvest, so it's easy for us coffee geeks to feel part of an exclusive club as we pass another commuter clutching a pint's worth of milky, chain-cafe coffee. Do they even know what they're missing, we wonder?

Instant coffee, super milky coffee, so-dark-it-tastes-burnt coffee and capsules have all been lumped together as the antithesis of the speciality coffee experience, where quality beans are carefully roasted and served by an obsessive barista.

So when multi-UK barista champ and roastery owner Maxwell Colonna-Dashwood of Colonna announced he was putting speciality coffee into capsules, it raised a few eyebrows.

'The thing is, the big companies who make capsule coffee want it to taste like an Italian espresso because that's what most people want,' says Max. *'And then when people who appreciate speciality coffee drink a cup made using that type of technology, they think the format is the issue, as opposed to the coffee.'*

'CAPSULES ARE ACTUALLY A PERFECT DELIVERY SYSTEM FOR SPECIALITY COFFEE'

'Capsules are actually a perfect delivery system for speciality coffee because, let's face it, most people are not baristas.

'The speciality scene has long focused on "freshly roasted and freshly ground", so one of the criticisms of capsules has been freshness, but we're focusing on green coffee, because we've found that if the green beans are roasted when very fresh that has the biggest impact on the cup of coffee. Much more so than if the beans are older when roasted and then freshly ground.'

'People have a lot of prejudice, and think that by making it more convenient you are dumbing it down, but it allows us to focus on a more interesting message. Because when I sell a bag of beans the conversation is all about how

> **'IF THE GREEN BEANS ARE ROASTED WHEN VERY FRESH IT HAS THE BIGGEST IMPACT ON THE CUP OF COFFEE – MORE THAN IF THE BEANS ARE OLDER WHEN ROASTED AND THEN FRESHLY GROUND'**

Maxwell Colonna-Dashwood

the consumer is going to brew it. However if we can do more of the making for the customer (by supplying it in capsules) then the narrative can be about the flavour and where it is from. It's an adventure that's similar to the experience people have with wine.'

Another speciality roaster seeing the opportunities in the capsule market is Will Little of Devon's Roastworks Coffee Co. who says: 'until a couple of months ago I had no interest in looking at capsules – I thought they were the Devil's work – but there's always been the challenge of how to get people who aren't into speciality coffee to drink better coffee. They're missing out on the gamut of flavours that naturally occur in coffee.

'Then I read James Hoffmann of Square Mile Coffee's blog about capsules and started doing some testing, because the growth rate for pods is something like double year-on-year, it's ridiculous. I thought, if we can nail this, we can get better coffee to millions – not hundreds – of consumers.

'There are a number of people doing non-speciality pods in the market with Nespresso dominating, so we bought everything we could in order to do a proper evaluation. There was one Nespresso pod – an Ethiopian which they don't call Ethiopian – which I thought was okay, but to me everything else came out bad. So I felt there was a big market for something more special.

'Finding a UK manufacturer who had just invested in a capsule filling line with a fancy pants Neuhaus Neotec grinder and the facilities to pack the pods in a nitrogen atmosphere was the next piece of luck.' And after a lot of research and development the pods were launched in August.

'I believe we've got our hands on the best compatible capsule in the market from a performance perspective, and the flavour of our capsules is great. We have a double AA grade varietal that's big, juicy and tastes of blackcurrants. I won't tell you that it's better than an espresso as it's a different drink.

'We're saying,"You've got one of those pod machines? Try something better". No-one has stepped into those premium pod shoes yet, so I'm really excited.'

YOUR JOURNEY STARTS HERE

CAFES

Coffee shops and cafes where you can drink top-notch speciality coffee. We've split the whole of the South West and South Wales into areas to help you find places near you.

ROASTERS

Meet the leading speciality coffee roasters in the region and discover where to source beans to use at home.

Finally, you'll discover More Good Cups and More Good Roasters at the end of each section.

MAPS

Every cafe and roaster has a number so you can find them either on the large fold-out map or the detailed city maps – all at the back of the guide.

Don't forget to let us know how you get on as you explore the best speciality cafes and roasters:

www.indycoffee.guide

🐦 @indycoffeeguide 📷 @indycoffeeguide

CAFES

UNCOMMON GROUND
COFFEE ROASTER

№ 8

1. WRIGHT'S FOOD EMPORIUM

Golden Grove Arms, Llanarthne, Carmarthenshire, Wales, SA32 8JU.

From coffee, to food, to wine, to all-round good vibes, or *many reasons to be cheerful* as manager Rich succinctly puts it, Wright's is a definite must-visit.

The old converted countryside pub has grown organically into a gourmet wonderland where you can breakfast like a king on bubble and squeak with poached eggs and salumi, lunch on nectarine, ewe's curd and pistachio salad and, come supper time, feast on dishes such as Cardigan Bay crab linguine. Oh, and there's always a groaning sideboard of custard slices and homemade cakes, as well as a deli counter so you can buy goodies-to-go.

INSIDER'S TIP
TRY THE SIGNATURE PORK BELLY CUBANO

All these eating occasions require good coffee, of course, which is provided with aplomb by Welsh Coffee Company, Coaltown, James Gourmet and Clifton, either as espresso or batch filter ['we prefer light, juicy roasts for our filter to highlight the coffee fruit,' says Rich].

Other liquid offerings include an unusually good selection of small scale, minimal intervention wines and casks so you can take your own bottles for filling. Delightful.

KEY ROASTER
Welsh Coffee Company

BREWING METHODS
Espresso, batch filter, cold brew

MACHINE
Rancilio

GRINDERS
Mazzer, Compak

OPENING HOURS
Mon 11am-7pm
Wed-Thur 9am-7pm
Fri-Sat 9am-late
Sun 11am-5pm

COFFEE BEANS AVAILABLE

SOYA MILK AVAILABLE

WIFI

CYCLE FRIENDLY

OUTDOOR SEATING

FAMILY FRIENDLY

DISABLED ACCESS

DOG FRIENDLY

www.wrightsfood.co.uk T: 01558 668929

Wright's Independent Food Emporium @wrightsfood @wrightsfood

№2. GINHAUS DELI

1 Market Street, Llandeilo, Carmarthenshire, Wales, SA19 6AH.

You don't have to be a gin (or coffee) fan to visit Ginhaus Deli, but it certainly helps. Because with over 320 gins from across the globe, Mike and Kate Kindred and team are certainly doing the juniper plant justice. Then there's the coffee, sourced from Coaltown Coffee Roasters down the road and served with the skill and care that runs throughout the enterprise.

The pair have turned this old pub into a treasure trove of good eating and drinking with a groaning deli counter of local cheeses and continental meats (the goodies turn up on platters for customers to wolf down at wine barrel tables), gin display and coffee bar. *'We were inspired by a place we visited in Italy,'* says Mike.

INSIDER'S TIP
PAIR YOUR COFFEE WITH ONE OF THE V POPULAR FRANGIPANE TARTS – THEY SELL 400 A WEEK

With gourmet pizzas on Friday and Saturday nights, monthly gin tasting boards and the introduction of V60s, it's not surprising to discover that Ginhaus is where Mike and Kate go on their night off.

KEY ROASTER
Coaltown Coffee Roasters

BREWING METHODS
Espresso, V60

MACHINE
La Spaziale S5 EKTA 2 group

GRINDERS
Anfim Milano, Mahlkonig Vario

OPENING HOURS
Mon-Thu
8am-5pm
Fri-Sat
8am-10pm

www.ginhaus.co.uk   T: 01558 823030

f Ginhaus Deli   🐦 @ginhausdeli   📷 @ginhaus1

№3. SQUARE PEG COFFEE HOUSE

29b Gower Road, Sketty, Swansea, Wales, SA2 9BX.

Proudly claiming the honour of being the first speciality coffee shop in Swansea, Square Peg has lots more to shout about besides originality.

Top-notch coffee (Clifton with guest roasts from Ozone among others) is served with skill by SCAE qualified barista Josh, alongside seriously good cafe food which is all made in-house. Homemade brownies jostle with Welsh bacon and homemade spicy beans for your attention, and the teas are as good as the coffee.

INSIDER'S TIP SQUARE PEG'S ITALIAN CHEF IS CREATING FOOD AS GOOD AS THE COFFEE

What's especially different about Square Peg is the focus on social enterprise that runs throughout. *'Our priority is people – building friendships with the community and further afield,'* says one of the owners, Matt Crome. *'We give our profits to support local causes as well as a charity for street children in Kenya. "Give back, give more, be different" – that's our ethos.'*

The cosy cafe is open early so it's a no brainer for your morning kick-start, plus, *'we do a mean avo on toast for brunch,'* smiles Matt.

KEY ROASTER
Clifton Coffee
Roasters

BREWING METHODS
Espresso, V60,
AeroPress,
cold brew

MACHINE
La Marzocco
Linea

GRINDERS
Mythos,
Compak R80

OPENING HOURS
Mon-Fri 8am-7pm
Sat 8am-5pm

 Gluten FREE

 COFFEE BEANS AVAILABLE

 SOYA MILK AVAILABLE

 WIFI

 CYCLE FRIENDLY

 OUTDOOR SEATING

 FAMILY FRIENDLY

 DISABLED ACCESS

www.squarepeg.org.uk T: 01792 206593

f Square Peg Coffee 🐦 @squarepegcoffee 📷 @squarepegcoffee

4. COFFEE PUNKS

32 The Kingsway, Swansea, Wales, SA1 5LE.

Bang in the centre of Swansea and part of The Kingsway redevelopment, Coffee Punks is one of the coffee shops leading the speciality revolution in the city.

It's also sporting a spanking new refurb, along with a trade up from the previous espresso machine to a La Marzocco Linea PB, and a new Saturday brunch menu, '*so it's all systems go*,' says manager and barista Paul.

INSIDER'S TIP: LOOK OUT FOR REGULAR ACOUSTIC, ROCK, ART AND POETRY GIGS

The house roast comes courtesy of much-loved James Gourmet and there's a focus on single origin coffees all year round, with regularly rotating guest coffees as well as cold brew. Drink it as espresso, via the AeroPress or as V60 – indoors or out front in the hubbub.

Plus, in the pursuit of excellence all the staff are SCAE certified and every coffee is weighed in and out. Bring it on.

KEY ROASTER
James Gourmet Coffee

BREWING METHODS
Espresso, pourover, AeroPress, cold brew

MACHINE
La Marzocco Linea PB

GRINDER
Mythos One Clima Pro

OPENING HOURS
Mon-Fri 9am-6pm
Sat 9am-5pm

www.coffeepunks.coffee   T: 07800 853705

f Coffee Punks   @coffeepunks   @coffeepunks

5. LEW'S COFFEE SHOP

Unit 5 Avocet House, 88 Station Road, Cardiff, CF14 2FG.

With its cracking local coffee, (mum's) homemade cakes and a lush Welsh welcome from owner Lewys, every neighbourhood should have a coffee shop like Lew's in Llandaff North.

It's a proper community cafe, and in addition to finding locals nattering over Coaltown cappuccinos on the cosy sofas, the community spirit is also embodied in the quirky décor of this homely hangout.

Colourful postcards from regulars' trips around the world decorate the back door, while unfamiliar coins and battered foreign notes from afar adorn the bar and creep up the wall. There's even a book in which Lew's fans declare their love for the cafe and its coffee.

INSIDER'S TIP STOCK UP ON LOCAL PRODUCERS' GOODIES: JAM, CRISPS AND COFFEE

Opening the shop nine years ago at just 19, Lew's had plenty of time to perfect his baristas skills, now passing on his wisdom to the young brigade of baristas. Try one of the expertly prepared espresso based drinks with a pistachio and salted caramel Cronut, or for serious indulgence add a side of warm waffles drizzled with maple syrup and ice cream.

KEY ROASTER
Coaltown Coffee Company

BREWING METHOD
Espresso

MACHINE
Nera 2 Group

GRINDER
San Marco SM90/A

OPENING HOURS
Mon-Sat 9am-5pm
Sun 11am-3pm

Gluten FREE

COFFEE BEANS AVAILABLE

SOYA MILK AVAILABLE

WIFI

CYCLE FRIENDLY

OUTDOOR seating

FAMILY FRIENDLY

DOG FRIENDLY

T: 02920 555560

f Lew's Coffee Shop   🐦 @lewscoffeeshop   📷 @lewscoffeeshop

6. LUFKIN COFFEE ROASTERS

183a Kings Road, Cardiff, CF11 9DF.

Tucked away in a charming little courtyard in Pontcanna, this coffee shop is the perfect excuse to stray from the city centre in order to discover one of Cardiff's liveliest indie suburbs.

Housed in a small wooden structure, alongside artist studios and a craft brewery, the coffee offering is as minimal as the contemporary design here, but that doesn't mean there's nothing to get buzzed about.

INSIDER'S TIP KEEP AN EYE OPEN FOR EXCITING COLLABORATIONS WITH PIPES BREWERY NEXT DOOR - LAST YEAR'S COFFEE PORTER WAS A SELL-OUT

Sourcing a rotation of seasonal single origin green beans, roasting them behind the bar and serving Lufkin's regulars with top-notch espresso, pourover and cold brew, along with cakes and sandwiches, is an impressive feat on the part of owners Dan and Frances.

Grab a stool at the brew bar and sample the latest batch while luxuriating in the waft of next week's coffee that's roasting just a few feet away. If the weather's good, take a pew in the outdoor seating area, custom designed and built by the local university's architecture programme, with something tasty sourced from the local farmers' market.

KEY ROASTER
Lufkin Coffee Roasters

BREWING METHODS
Espresso, pourover, cold brew

MACHINE
La Spaziale S1

GRINDER
Mazzer Luigi

OPENING HOURS
Wed-Sat
9.30am-5.30pm
Sun 9.30am-4pm

 Gluten FREE

 COFFEE BEANS AVAILABLE

 SOYA MILK AVAILABLE

 WIFI

 CYCLE FRIENDLY

 OUTDOOR SEATING

 FAMILY FRIENDLY

 DISABLED ACCESS

 DOG FRIENDLY

www.lufkincoffee.com   T: 07570 811764

f Lufkin Coffee Roasters   ⬤ @lufkincoffee   ⬤ @lufkincoffee

7. THE PLAN CAFE

28-29 Morgan Arcade, Cardiff, Wales, CF10 1AF.

Tucked away in a beautiful listed building in the heart of Morgan Arcade, The Plan is Cardiff's original speciality coffee shop.

Head barista Trevor Hyam has been the force behind the brew here since 2007, making it one of the first places in Wales to serve artisan, third wave coffee.

A 2010 UK Barista Championship finalist, Trevor now trains the team of budding baristas at the bustling cafe, between writing up the latest tasting notes, perfecting the ultimate cold brew recipe and serving the house coffee from James Gourmet in a variety of styles.

INSIDER'S TIP CHOOSE FROM A VAST AND EVER-CHANGING SELECTION OF IN-SEASON SINGLE ORIGINS ON FRENCH PRESS

With large windows and a second floor balcony, there's plenty of bright and airy space in which to enjoy your coffee – with something delicious from the extensive breakfast and lunch menu. There are stacks of options for veggie and vegan visitors, local and organically-sourced produce featured throughout and some tip-top baked treats too – the perfect excuse to order a second flat white.

KEY ROASTER
James Gourmet Coffee

BREWING METHODS
Espresso, french press, batch brew, cold brew

MACHINE
Astoria Plus 4U

GRINDERS
Modified Anfim Super Caimano, Bunn G3

OPENING HOURS
Mon-Sat 8.45am-5pm
Sun 10am-4pm

www.theplancafe.co.uk T: 02920 398764

f The Plan Café Cardiff 🐦 @theplancafe 📷 @the_plan_cafe

CLIFTON
COFFEE
ROASTERS
CLIFTONCOFFEE.CO.UK

Great coffee is everywhere. But a great partner
for your business is harder to find.

With over 16 years experience in supplying the hospitality trade, we
work with the finest equipment manufacturers in the world to ensure
each and every cup of coffee you serve is the very best it can be.

Sourcing. Roasting. Educating. Engineering

www.cliftoncoffee.co.uk
sales@cliftoncoffee.co.uk | 01179 820252

  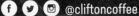 @cliftoncoffee

№8. UNCOMMON GROUND COFFEE ROASTERY

10-12 Royal Arcade, Cardiff, Wales, CF10 1AE.

When Ian and Paul Hayman grew tired of the nine-to-five, the brothers blended the creative credentials and coffee wisdom from their previous roles – Ian worked in photography, Paul managed a Caffè Nero – to open their dream coffee shop, Uncommon Ground.

INSIDER'S TIP — GRAB A BULGING BREAKFAST BURRITO OR A CAKE MADE BY IAN AND PAUL'S MUM

Pitching up in Cardiff's proudly indie Royal Arcade, Ian and Paul created a quirky social space – with copper kettle lights hanging from the ceiling and exposed brick walls – where caffeine tourists congregate, students hunch over laptops and business people break their day for a speciality brew.

The plan to roast their own coffee in-store from the get-go was quashed by sky-high costs, however Leeds' North Star have done a sterling job stocking the grinder with sensational single origins until the guys' own roastery starts pumping at the end of 2016.

KEY ROASTER
North Star Coffee Roasters

BREWING METHODS
Espresso, V60, AeroPress, cold brew

MACHINE
La Spaziale

GRINDER
Anfim Caimano OD

OPENING HOURS
Mon-Sat 7.30am-6.30pm
Sun 10am-5.30pm

Gluten FREE

COFFEE BEANS AVAILABLE

SOYA MILK AVAILABLE

WIFI

CYCLE FRIENDLY

OUTDOOR SEATING

FAMILY FRIENDLY

www.uncommon-ground.co.uk

f Uncommon Ground Coffee Roastery　🐦 @_uncommonground　📷 @_uncommonground

№9. THE LITTLE MAN COFFEE COMPANY

Ivor House, Bridge Street, Cardiff, Wales, CF10 2EE.

© Amelia Holdsworth

After 10 years working in late night bars and clubs across the UK, Rob Cooper decided to trade in the 5am finishes for 5am starts when he opened The Little Man Coffee Company in October 2014.

Inspired by San Francisco's speciality scene and the rarity of a great cup in the capital, Rob acquired what was a former 1960s post office and transformed it into a contemporary space for the city's creative folk to plan and meet over coffee and basement-made cake.

INSIDER'S TIP CHECK OUT THE CONVERTED BANK VAULT DOWNSTAIRS – FOR MEETINGS, CLASSES AND CREATIVE EVENTS

'It seemed the time was right to open a speciality shop,' explains Rob, 'people were moving away from spending time in pubs and moving towards a fresh cafe culture.'

Instead of getting into bed with just one roastery, Little Man features a rotating line-up of 18 roasters from across the UK, giving regulars the opportunity to sample a hefty selection of coffees. The fully licensed venue also harbours a bottle shop in its belly – make sure to stock up on craft beers in the basement.

KEY ROASTERS
Coaltown Coffee Roasters,
North Star Coffee Roasters,
Neighbourhood,
Welsh Coffee Company

BREWING METHODS
Espresso, V60, Aero-Press, Chemex, cold brew, french press

MACHINE
La Marzocco, Linea AV

GRINDERS
Compak E8 x 2,
Compak R80

OPENING HOURS
Mon-Fri
7am-9pm
Sat 8am-9pm
Sun 8am-5pm

Gluten FREE

COFFEE BEANS AVAILABLE

SOYA MILK AVAILABLE

WIFI

CYCLE FRIENDLY

COFFEE COURSES AVAILABLE

FAMILY FRIENDLY

DISABLED ACCESS

www.littlemancoffee.co.uk   T: 07933 844234

f The Little Man Coffee Co   🐦 @littlemancoffee   📷 @littlemancoffee

Nº 10. KIN+ILK

1 Capital Quarter, Tyndall Street, Cardiff, Wales, CF10 4BZ.

A fresh venue on Cardiff's burgeoning coffee scene, KIN+ILK CAPITAL QUARTER was such a success when it opened its doors in January 2016 that a second venue, KIN+ILK PONTCANNA popped up just a couple of months later on the city's Cathedral Road.

Although the Pontcanna cafe bar is your go-to for weekend brunching and cappuccino catch-ups, the original coffee shop is more about espresso-to-go and lunchtime caffeine fixes. Slap bang in office central, this is the kind of place where you can bury your head in a laptop with a good filter or swing by on your way to work.

INSIDER'S TIP CHECK OUT THE REGULAR EVENTS AND POP UPS

Talented baristas excel at coffee chat and use Bristol's Clifton Coffee, with its unique El Salvador Finca El Izote single origin, especially selected for KIN+ILK's two sites.

The sandwiches, baked goodies and sweet treats are all sourced from local producers, maintaining the cafe's keen focus on supporting Cardiff's creative and business community.

KEY ROASTER
Clifton Coffee Roasters

BREWING METHODS
Espresso, filter, Chemex, drip

MACHINE
La Marzocco

GRINDERS
Mythos, Mahlkonig

OPENING HOURS
Mon-Fri
7.30am-6pm

www.kinandilk.com   T: 02922 401809

KIN + ILK Capital Quarter   @kinandilk   @kinandilk

11. NEW ENGLAND COFFEE HOUSE

1 Digbeth Street, Stow-on-the-Wold, Cheltenham, Gloucestershire, GL54 1BN.

A simple sign above the beautiful Cotswold stone building is all that New England Coffee House in Stow-on-the-Wold needs, because the intoxicating aroma of freshly roasted coffee that wafts from this charming speciality shop is enough to keep the caffeine fans coming.

INSIDER'S TIP SOUND THE KLAXON - OWNER DAVID HAS PERFECTED THE ESPRESSO MARTINI!

The welcoming combination of original 17th century features, cosy leather sofas and touches of country house glamour invite you to spend a little longer over the small batch coffee. There's a selection of locally made cakes and homemade smoothies to complement the espresso-based brew offering too.

To make sure the perfect cup is served every time, the in-house espresso blend changes with the season, so visitors can look forward to new tasting notes on a return trip. Traditional non-homogenised milk from a mile down the road ensures the finished product is of the most authentic - and delicious - quality.

KEY ROASTER
Stow Town Coffee

BREWING METHODS
Espresso, filter

MACHINE
Fracino Contempo

GRINDERS
Ceado E37, Mazzer

OPENING HOURS
Mon-Fri
8.30am-5pm
Sat-Sun
9am-5pm

 Gluten FREE

 COFFEE BEANS AVAILABLE

 SOYA MILK AVAILABLE

 WIFI

 DOG FRIENDLY

www.newenglandcoffeehouse.co.uk   T: 01451 831171

f New England Coffee House   @newengcoffeehse

12. BOSTON TEA PARTY

45-49 Clarence Street, Cheltenham, Gloucestershire, GL50 3JS.

A big old building steeped in history, a counter piled high with the morning's fresh bakes, lots of space and quirky seating to lounge in, oh and a damn good cup of coffee – there's no doubt that Cheltenham's new hangout is one of the Boston's bunch.

Whatever your speciality style, the Clarence Street venue is perfectly positioned slap bang in the centre of town for pre-work piccolos, mid-shopping flat white fuel-ups and lazy late afternoon lattes. And Extract Coffee and a team of trained baristas are on hand for your personalised caffeine hit.

INSIDER'S TIP BOSTON'S SMOOTHIES AND ICED COFFEES ARE NOW MADE WITH AVOCADO INSTEAD OF FRAPPE POWDERS – THE SAME SILKY SWEET TASTE BUT NO SWEETENERS

Once you've chosen from the extensive drinks list, the next challenge is whittling down the free-range foodie offering. From Instagram famous brunch plates to badass bacon jam burgers and fruit scones as big as your face, everything on the menu is ethically sourced and made in-store each day.

KEY ROASTER
Extract Coffee Roasters

BREWING METHODS
Espresso, Marco batch brew

MACHINE
La Marzocco Linea Classic

GRINDERS
Mazzer Majors

OPENING HOURS
Mon-Sun 7am-9pm

www.bostonteaparty.co.uk   T: 01242 573935

Boston Tea Party Cafés   @btpcafes   @btpcafes

№13. THE COFFEE DISPENSARY

18 Regent Street, Cheltenham, Gloucestershire, GL50 1HE.

With chemical equations etched on the bright white walls, a filter board scribbled with exotic destinations and wooden shelves heaving with the latest brewing gear and roasters' yield, owner Gary Marshall's passion for the science of speciality certainly shows in The Coffee Dispensary's Scandi interior.

Inspired by Copenhagen's thriving coffee culture, this stylish spot on Cheltenham's Regent Street is a mecca for Gloucestershire's brew buffs. Whether you're after a flawless flat white or a cracking local cold brew, the attractive line-up of exclusively single origin roasts on the grinders means no two pilgrimages to this coffee haven will be the same.

INSIDER'S TIP
FANCY A CHANGE FROM THE STANDARD FLAT WHITE? TRY LOCAL COLD BREW, ANTLER & BIRD

Those making the trip should keep a check on The Coffee Dispensary's social media as Gary and team hold regular cupping sessions and one-off events such as speciality film screenings and talks with farmers and roasters. And don't forget to fuel-up for the onward journey with a homemade cake or tray bake from local bakery Hetty's Tea Party.

KEY ROASTERS
Extract Coffee Roasters, The Barn

BREWING METHODS
Espresso, V60, AeroPress, syphon

MACHINE
Sanremo Opera

GRINDERS
EK43, K30

OPENING HOURS
Mon-Sat
8.30am-5.30pm
Sun 9.30am-5pm

www.the-coffee-dispensary.co.uk   T: 01242 260597

The Coffee Dispensary   @coffeedispenser   @the_coffee_dispensary

14. BREW & BAKE

217 Bath Road, Cheltenham, Gloucestershire, GL53 7NA.

It's been a busy year for Brew & Bake on Cheltenham's Bath Road. No doubt fuelled by the quality brews on the bar, owner (and former chef) Mark Conway has revved up the brunch offerings from weekend treat to everyday indulgence, added more monthly supper clubs in the comfy coffee shop and launched a town centre pop-up that's pairing gourmet grub with top-notch coffee.

It may have been non-stop, but you'd never tell, as the friendly team of baristas have continued to crank out fabulous brews with the house beans from Ue (the only wood-fired roaster in the UK) for the army of loyal locals and coffee tourists who fill this neighbourhood spot.

INSIDER'S TIP FIND GUEST ROASTS FROM ACROSS THE COUNTRY MAKING AN APPEARANCE ON THE QUIRKY FILTER BOARD

Come armed with a healthy appetite, as these guys take cake pretty seriously – when *GBBO*'s on telly, you'll find the kitchen crew tackling the technical challenge each week – so good luck avoiding the sweet temptations piled high on the counter. There's also a massive selection of homemade sausage rolls and sarnies for savoury snackers, with creative combos such as kale pesto, chargrilled courgette and grated carrot.

KEY ROASTER
Ue Coffee Roasters

BREWING METHODS
Espresso, V60, Chemex, AeroPress

MACHINE
La Marzocco Linea

GRINDER
Super Jolly on demand

OPENING HOURS
Mon-Sat 7am-6pm
Sun 10am-3pm

www.brewandbake.coffee   T 01242 580875
f Brew & Bake   🐦 @brewandbakehq   © @brewandbake_hq

15. STAR ANISE ARTS CAFE

Painswick Inn, 1 Gloucester Street, Stroud, Gloucestershire, GL5 1QG.

Whether you're a yoga master, funk and soul follower or have just discovered a new found love of flamenco, there's always something exciting to get stuck into at this lively hub.

And it's not just the line-up of live music, supper clubs and creative events which keep the customers coming back to the friendly family cafe, as there's also an impressive bill of wholesome food and top-notch coffee to fuel activities.

INSIDER'S TIP
THE DAILY SOURDOUGH IS MADE USING A 30-YEAR-OLD SAN FRANCISCO STARTER

While local roaster Extract keeps the Sanremo machine ticking over, local suppliers stock the kitchen with gorgeous organic ingredients. At lunchtime, try the house speciality of brown rice sushi with avocado and tempura prawns then, come afternoon, pair your coffee with a generous slab of chocolate and avocado torte.

Tucked away just off Stroud's busy high street, there's also space to find a little coffee calm here. We'd recommend a glass of something good from the organic wine and craft beer selection in the sunshine.

KEY ROASTER
Extract Coffee
Roasters

BREWING METHOD
Espresso

MACHINE
Sanremo

GRINDER
Sanremo

OPENING HOURS
Mon-Fri 8am-5pm
Sat 8.30am-5pm

www.staraniseartscafe.com T: 01453 840021

f Star Anise Arts Cafe 🐦 @staranisecafe @ @staranisecafe

16. THE COFFEE GONDOLA

At festivals and snow-sports venues.

We've seen some quirky spaces serving speciality coffee but The Coffee Gondola's converted ski lift has got to be one of the coolest.

Sourcing a ski gondola to convert was no easy feat for Tom Steggall and Josie Adams, the snow and coffee mad couple behind the mobile venue. *'We emailed every ski resort in Europe and then, with no luck, tried every resort in the world,'* explains Tom. *'We struck it lucky when Whistler in Canada was auctioning off 11 of its cabins and after a 2am bidding war, #84 was ours.'*

INSIDER'S TIP FORMER PRIVATE CHEFS, TOM AND JOSIE ARE CRANKING OUT HOMEMADE ALTERNATIVE MILKS, MARSHMALLOWS AND COFFEE SYRUPS

Shipping the gondola to the UK and converting it into a functioning coffee shop gave Tom and Josie time to brush up their barista skills with a little help from family friend – and Reads Coffee owner – Giles Dick-Read. *'We gained invaluable experience working in Reads Roastbox for the summer,'* says Tom.

Scrubbed up and ready for action, look out for #84 fuelling the UK's festival goers with top-notch Clifton coffee at events throughout the summer. While in winter, you'll find Tom and Josie treating the Alp's holidaymakers to a well-earned speciality brew at the bottom of a mountain.

KEY ROASTER
Clifton Coffee Roasters

BREWING METHODS
Espresso, filter, cold brew

MACHINE
Fracino Contempo duel fuel

GRINDER
Compak E8

OPENING HOURS
As per event

 Gluten FREE

 COFFEE BEANS AVAILABLE

 SOYA MILK AVAILABLE

 CYCLE FRIENDLY

 OUTDOOR Seating

 FAMILY Friendly

 DISABLED ACCESS

DOG FRIENDLY

www.thecoffeegondola.com   T: 07871 328490

f The Coffee Gondola   🐦 @gondolacoffee   📷 @thecoffeegondola

BRISTOL, BATH & SOMERSET

THE RIVER HOUSE
№ 41

THE RIVER HOUSE

№17. ESTE KITCHEN

7 Greenbank Road, Easton, Bristol, BS5 6EZ.

'*Coffee is part of your culture when you are Colombian and Brazilian,*' explains the family team at Este Kitchen. So it was only natural, after spending the summers of her childhood frolicking around the family coffee farm in Anserma, Caldas, Colombia, that Sooz and her partner Sol would embrace the coffee tradition when they set up their own business.

After spending endless hours converting a run-down ex-chippy into a bright and welcoming space, the duo opened Este Kitchen in Bristol's Easton in April 2016.

INSIDER'S TIP GRAB AN OUTDOOR SEAT ON THE WEEKEND FOR A LAZY BRUNCH SESH

Though Grandma's beans aren't on the grinder yet, a rotating selection of down-the-road roaster, Extract's house blend and single origins are keeping visitors expertly caffeinated until co-operative farming rules and regs are ironed out.

A vibrant menu of healthy Latino-inspired breakfast, brunch and lunch dishes makes Este Kitchen worth venturing from the city centre for, and the sweet selection of bakes decorating the bar – courtesy of Sol's family and local bakers – means that something edible with your elevenses brew is a must.

KEY ROASTER
Extract Coffee Roasters

BREWING METHOD
Espresso

MACHINE
Sanremo Zoe

GRINDER
Mythos One Clima-Pro

OPENING HOURS
Tue-Sat 9am-5pm
Sun 10am-4pm

Gluten FREE

COFFEE BEANS AVAILABLE

SOYA MILK AVAILABLE

WIFI

OUTDOOR Seating

FAMILY FRiENdly

---

www.estekitchen.com   T: 01173 789744

f Este Kitchen   🐦 @estekitchen   📷 @estekitchen

18. SPICER+COLE

16 The Promenade, Gloucester Road, Bristol, BS7 8AE.

It may have only opened its doors in March 2016 but Spicer+Cole's third casual dining coffee shop – this one on indie Gloucester Road – has already proved a hit with the melting pot of locals frequenting the bustling street.

INSIDER'S TIP BOOK THE PRIVATE DINING AREA FOR UP TO EIGHT CHUMS FOR A SATURDAY BRUNCH SESH

Like its sister venues on Queen Square Avenue and in Clifton Village, the baby of the bunch offers a cracking cup of espresso based coffee from local roaster Extract, alongside a refreshing menu of brunch and lunch faves that change daily.

Dedication to the brew has been cranked up a level at the new digs, as head barista Renaud has just qualified as an AST trainer and is passing on the passion to his legacy of shot-pullers. The fresh machine and grinder set-up has also been hand selected to allow more control over each cup.

A mish-mash of communal benches, corner tables and outside seating means the spacious venue is a great spot in which to squirrel away with the laptop, a coffee and a slab of homemade cake, or meet friends for a long, lazy lunch.

KEY ROASTER
Extract Coffee Roasters

BREWING METHODS
Espresso, cold brew

MACHINE
La Marzocco Linea PB

GRINDERS
Mythos x 2, Sanremo

OPENING HOURS
Mon-Sat
8.30am-5.30pm
Sun 9am-5.30pm

Gluten FREE

SOYA MILK AVAILABLE

WIFI

OUTDOOR SEATING

DISABLED ACCESS

www.spicerandcole.co.uk   T: 01179 247628

f Spicer and Cole   🐦 @spicerandcole   📷 @spicerandcole

MAP 19. TRADEWIND ESPRESSO

118 Whiteladies Road, Clifton, Bristol, BS8 2RP.

Celebrating its first birthday in September 2016, it's been a successful first year for Tradewind Espresso, the coffee shop counterpart to Bristol based micro-roaster Roasted Rituals.

Owners Patrick and Tahi Grant-Sturgis and head roaster Courtney Taylor Jackson have created a contemporary space in which to enjoy the fruits of their roaster – try the Highground house blend or mull over a number of rotating single origins. Courtney also encourages the local community to delve deeper into speciality coffee, holding monthly cupping sessions and offering customers first dibs on the latest batch in-store.

Their own-roasted coffee is accompanied by a menu of wholesome, home-cooked food that'll see visitors through from early breakfast to late lunch. Menus change with the season; in summer there are rainbow-hued Buddha bowls, while in winter the spiced kedgeree is the go-to, with french toast, chargrilled peaches and honeycomb mascarpone a fave all year round.

Rustic cakes and bakes stacking the counter also come courtesy of Tradewind's busy little kitchen, with the spectacular spiced buns delivered daily from Farro – an old neighbour from the roaster's early days at the Whiteladies farmers' market.

KEY ROASTER
Roasted Rituals

BREWING METHODS
Espresso, V60, french press

MACHINE
La Marzocco Linea PB

GRINDERS
Mazzer Robur x 2, EK43

OPENING HOURS
Mon-Sat 8am-5pm
Sun 9am-4pm

INSIDER'S TIP IN SUMMER, GRAB A ROASTED RITUALS COLD BREW AND MAKE FOR THE COURTYARD

www.tradewindespresso.com T: 07855 380561

f Tradewind Espresso 🐦 @tradewind118 📷 @tradewindespresso

20. MOCKINGBIRD

58 Alma Vale Road, Clifton, Bristol, BS8 2HS.

Come armed with a healthy appetite – and an expandable waistband – to this Deep South inspired eatery, as there's fat chance you'll end up visiting *just* for coffee.

With sweet potato hash, smashed avo, and Southern buttermilk biscuits with sausage gravy on the menu, we're thanking our lucky stars that this bright and modern haunt on Bristol's Alma Vale Road serves its badass brunch from breakfast through to lunch.

After an epic feasting sesh you'll want to perk up with a quality coffee, and owner Oliver Cooper's got that covered with a seductive selection of seasonal single origins from Extract and Round Hill. Take your pick between espresso and V60, or when the weather is warm try it iced.

INSIDER'S TIP
PICK UP A BUNCH OF FRESH FLOWERS FROM THE IN-STORE FLORIST

If you're craving a sweet fix after devouring the sandwich of the week, the house special, Mississippi mud, is a must. Packed with condensed milk and a sprinkle of chocolate, this caffeinated treat is your speciality alternative to sickly sweet syrup lattes.

KEY ROASTER
Extract Coffee Roasters

BREWING METHODS
Espresso, V60

MACHINE
La Spaziale S2

GRINDER
Mahlkonig K30 Vario

OPENING HOURS
Mon 9am-12pm
Tue-Sat 9am-4pm
Sun 10am-2pm

www.mockingbirdcafe.tumblr.com   T: 07734 666020

f Mockingbird   @mockingbirdalma   @mockingbirdbristol

21. BAKESMITHS

65 Whiteladies Road, Clifton, Bristol, BS8 2LY.

If you've enjoyed feeding your face with the Cakesmiths handmade cakes sold at good cafes across the South West, you'll definitely want to make a pilgrimage to its new baking mothership on Whiteladies Road in Bristol.

INSIDER'S TIP JUST ACROSS THE ROAD FROM THE EVERYMAN THEATRE, IT'LL SOON OPEN IN THE EVENINGS TOO

The large and airy Bakesmiths cafe-come-bakery-come-roaster bakes its own bread – eight different loaves each day – along with a whole range of creative cakes and sweet confections. Like the breads, the cakes change regularly, and recent faves include a rhubarb and custard loaf cake and peach and rosemary polenta cake. 'We like to think we're the edgy cake company,' beams owner Tom, who set up the Cakesmiths business with sister George 12 years ago after selling his Revival coffee shop on Corn Street in the city.

Tom's come full circle back to coffee and in addition to paying serious attention to how it serves its Clifton Coffee, Bakesmiths is also roasting its own on a test roaster right in the cafe. It provides great theatre, which, with the open bakery and the upstairs demo kitchen (look out for regular baking demos) means it's all too easy to spend the entire day here.

KEY ROASTER
Clifton Coffee Roasters

BREWING METHODS
Espresso, filter

MACHINE
La Marzocco Linea

GRINDER
Compak E8

OPENING HOURS
Mon-Fri 8am-5pm
Sat 9am-5pm
Sun 10am-4pm

 Gluten FREE
 COFFEE BEANS AVAILABLE
 SOYA MILK AVAILABLE
 WIFI
 OUTDOOR seating
 FAMILY FRIENDLY

www.bakesmiths.co.uk T: 01179 735644
f Bakesmiths @bakesmithshq @bakesmiths_hq

22. BREW COFFEE COMPANY

45 Whiteladies Road, Clifton, Bristol, BS8 2LS.

If you want to get stuck into some serious alfresco brunching in Bristol, Brew is your go-to spot for avo and smoked salmon topped sourdough, maple toasted oats and plates laden with poached eggs and smoked bacon.

INSIDER'S TIP: TRY THE AFFOGATO OF DOUBLE ESPRESSO OVER ICE CREAM, TOPPED WITH HOMEMADE HONEYCOMB

It's not just the delicious dishes coming from the tiny kitchen that the guys here are bossing, the speciality brew's pretty good too, with a cracking seasonal house blend from local roaster Clifton on espresso, alongside a rotating guest single origin filter. Ask one of the clued-up baristas behind the custom yellow La Marzocco for their tasting notes on the latest bean.

There's plenty of space in this modern cafe to spend time over your brew. Pull up one of the wooden chairs inside and browse the local artwork or watch the goings-on on indie HQ Whiteladies Road from the cluster of tables on the decking.

KEY ROASTER
Clifton Coffee Roasters

BREWING METHODS
Espresso, pourover

MACHINE
La Marzocco Linea PB

GRINDER
Mythos One

OPENING HOURS
Mon-Fri 7.30am-7pm
Sat 8am-7pm
Sun 9am-6pm

www.brewcoffeecompany.co.uk T: 01179 732842

f Brew Coffee Company   @brewcc   @brewcc

23. PINKMANS

85 Park Street, Bristol, BS1 5PJ.

You'll probably want to set aside a whole day for this one because once you've encountered the bliss that is the Pinkmans bakery counter, we can guarantee you'll be back later.

And there's every reason to make multiple pit stops at this working bakery, as from breakfast through to lunch and supper, the carb-laden goodies stocking the counter morph from plump pain au raisins and savoury pinwheels to Nutella stuffed sour-dough-nuts for elevenses, and late night puttanesca pizzas.

With such high foodie standards, only great coffee will suffice, and it's delivered by a crew of skilled baristas, the latest bluetooth kit from Cimbali and beans via Cornwall's Freehand Coffee Roasters.

INSIDER'S TIP BARBECUE BEANS, CHORIZO EGGS AND A SIDE ORDER OF CUSTARD DIPPED BRIOCHE? WE'RE IN

Grab a pew on one of the wooden feasting tables and take time over a signature foccacia and a single origin pourover – or an espresso martini if it's been one of those days – and watch the bakers working their magic on the loaves, tarts and treats for the city's busy workers to pick up on the way home.

KEY ROASTER
Freehand Coffee Roasters

BREWING METHODS
Espresso, filter

MACHINE
Cimbali 100

GRINDER
Cimbali Magnum on demand

OPENING HOURS
Mon 7.30am-7pm
Tue-Sat 7.30am-10pm
Sun and bank holidays 9am-6pm

www.pinkmans.co.uk   T: 01174 032040

f Pinkmans Bakery   @pinkmansbakery   @pinkmansbakery

24. LITTLE VICTORIES

7 Gaol Ferry Steps, Wapping Wharf, Bristol, BS1 6WE.

With their experience running one of Bristol's flagship speciality shops and a neat spot in the city's coolest new development, there was no doubt that the second venture from the guys behind Small Street Espresso was going to be an instant caffeine hit.

Just as at its sister cafe, coffee is given serious attention at the new Wapping Wharf venue. A dedicated espresso bar by day, sample the sterling selection of beans from Clifton as espresso, Chemex or cold brew. Come evening, the coffee cocktails, craft beers and organic wines start rolling, along with a line-up of artisan charcuterie and British cheeses worth fighting friends over.

INSIDER'S TIP LOOK OUT FOR COFFEE, CRAFT BEER AND FOOD MATCHING EVENTS

Unlike its older sibling, there's plenty of space to stick around at this stylish harbourside hangout. High ceilings, industrial style decor and an epic menu-board-come-art-installation make an ideal setting for lazing with a good brew and a slice of something sweet from the local bakeries stocking the eye-catching counter.

KEY ROASTER
Clifton Coffee Roasters

BREWING METHODS
Espresso, Chemex, cold brew

MACHINE
Black Eagle Gravitech

GRINDERS
Mythos x 3, EK43

OPENING HOURS
Mon-Tue 7.30am-4.30pm
Wed-Fri 7.30am-9pm
Sat 9.30am-9pm
Sun 9.30am-4.30pm

www.littlevics.co.uk

f Little Victories   @littlevicsbris   @littlevicsbris

25. MOKOKO

2 Gaol Ferry Steps, Wapping Wharf, Bristol, BS1 6WE.

Taking all the best bits from its flagship coffee emporium in Bath, and supersizing the slick speciality coffee and rustic bakery offering for its first Bristol venue, Mokoko's new digs on Wapping Wharf are a big little brother in the Jacob's Coffee House family.

From the open plan coffee bar through to the working kitchen, there's a mismatch of seating styles for every coffee drinking occasion.

INSIDER'S TIP EYE CANDY ALERT: THE MUSTARD YELLOW ESPRESSO MACHINES ARE SHOWSTOPPERS

Whether you're picking the baristas' brains from one of the tall stools at the brew bar, indulging in a spot of sociable coffee chat over lunch at a communal bench, or burying your nose in a book at the stainless steel window tables with a filter, you'll find your niche in the Scandinavian-style space.

Mull over the anything-but-average coffee menu – featuring two espressos, a guest filter and concoctions such as the cold brew espresso tonic – before selecting something delicious from the self-serve bakery benches for lunch. We like the apple and Somerset cider number for an afternoon pick-me-up.

KEY ROASTERS
Gardelli, La Cabra, Easy José

BREWING METHODS
Espresso, V60, Kalita Wave, Chemex

MACHINES
Conti Monte Carlo x 2

GRINDERS
Compak R120, Compak E10 – Conic RS Lucidate, Compak E8 & E6

OPENING HOURS
Mon-Sun
7.30am-6.30pm

 Gluten FREE

 COFFEE BEANS AVAILABLE

 SOYA MILK AVAILABLE

 WIFI

 CYCLE FRIENDLY

 OUTDOOR SEATING

 FAMILY FRIENDLY

 DISABLED ACCESS

www.mokokocoffee.com T: 01179 290177

@mokokocoffee @mokokocoffee

№26. JUST GROUND COFFEE KIOSK

Centre Promenade, City Centre, Bristol, BS1 4ST.

It may be one of Bristol's teeniest coffee haunts, but size definitely isn't an issue when it comes to the speciality brew at Just Ground Coffee Kiosk on the city's Centre Promenade.

With a lip-smacking line up of espresso based drinks, Extract's house blend stocking the grinder and a guest single origin to tempt visitors' tastebuds, this is your go-to for a mean brew on the move.

INSIDER'S TIP ON TWO WHEELS? CYCLISTS GET A COFFEE DISCOUNT

Acquiring the kooky kiosk in 2014, owner Arrow Jie upped the formerly Fairtrade coffee offering to speciality standards. *'The coffee tastes better and the ethos is just the same,'* enthuses Arrow. And it's this passion for the bean that keeps Just Ground's loyal regulars returning. *'We encourage the customers to discuss the extraction time of their coffee with us so that they know which tiny elements affect the taste. And we'll give impromptu latte art lessons if you ask nicely,'* he smiles.

Then pull up a chair at one of the pavement tables and get stuck into an artisan pastry or a warm sausage roll from Bristol's Dawson's and Farro bakeries.

KEY ROASTER
Extract Coffee Roasters

BREWING METHOD
Espresso

MACHINE
Sanremo Zoe

GRINDERS
Mahlkonig K30, Sanremo SR60

OPENING HOURS
Mon-Fri
6.30am-5.30pm
Sat 9am-5pm

www.justground.co.uk T: 07827 925807

f Just Ground Coffee Kiosk   @just_ground

27. PLAYGROUND COFFEE HOUSE

45 St Nicholas Street, Bristol, BS1 1TP.

It may be stocking the hottest new roasters on the speciality scene and harbouring some of the slickest brewing gear around, but there's still plenty of room for fun and games at this cosy little coffee house on St Nicholas Street.

INSIDER'S TIP: CHECK FABIAN'S BREWING VIDS ON THE WEBSITE FOR V60 AND AEROPRESS TIPS

Sourcing a selection of the world's finest beans from a constantly evolving cast of guest roasters, co-owner Fabian and his skilled squad of baristas can often be found playing around with new flavours and serve styles in search of the ultimate cup. Visitors can enjoy up to three filters and two constantly changing espressos on the menu at any time, as well as an intriguing range of teas, some hand sourced by Fabian's partner Lilly from her native Greece.

Drinks are served with a side of nostalgia, in the form of a set of swings replacing window seats and over a hundred retro board games with which to challenge fellow caffeine fiends. There's also a delicious range of baked goodies such as brownies and tray bakes from Lilly if you're after something sweet to accompany.

KEY ROASTER
Multi

BREWING METHODS
Espresso, V60, AeroPress, syphon

MACHINE
La Marzocco Linea

GRINDERS
Mahlkonig K30 Twin, Mahlkonig Colombia, Mahlkonig Vario

OPENING HOURS
Mon-Fri 8am-6pm
Sat 10.30am-6.30pm
Sun 11.30pm-4.30pm

www.playgroundcoffee.co.uk   T: 01173 290720

f Playground Coffee House   🐦 @playgroundcofco   ✉ @playgroundcoffeehouse

№28. SMALL STREET ESPRESSO

23 Small Street, Bristol, BS1 1DW.

One of the originals on the Bristol speciality scene, Small Street Espresso has been fuelling the city's brew buffs from its pocket-sized coffee shop since 2012.

There may only be a couple of benches up for grabs in this cosy, bare-brick-walled space – although an extension last year added a couple more pews – however, don't be fooled by its size as there's plenty of choice when it comes to coffee.

INSIDER'S TIP GRAB A 'HIT-AND-GO' - A COFFEE FOR THE ROAD AND A GUEST ESPRESSO WHILE YOU WAIT

Cottoning on to the spike in speciality interest a few years ago, the guys at Small Street not only offer a top-notch house blend from local roasters Clifton but also a sweet selection of single origins courtesy of guest roasters such as Yallah, Round Hill and Extract.

Super friendly staff and a loyal band of regulars make this a must-visit on a coffee tour of the city. A good selection of Hart's Bakery sarnies, seriously good choccie brownies and beans 'n' brewing equipment to take home are an added bonus.

KEY ROASTER
Clifton Coffee Roasters

BREWING METHODS
Espresso, cold brew, AeroPress

MACHINE
La Marzocco FB-80

GRINDERS
Mythos x 2, Mahlkonig Tanzania

OPENING HOURS
Mon-Fri
7.30am-4.30pm
Sat 9.30am-4.30pm

www.smallstreetespresso.co.uk

f Small St. Espresso 🐦 @smallstespresso @ @smallstespresso

29. BEARPIT SOCIAL

Container 1, St James Barton Underpass (The Bearpit), Bristol, BS1 3LE.

One of the more unusual coffee stops in Bristol, the Bearpit Social is a cheerful find in the big roundabout-come-hole-in-the-road of the same name.

A busy thoroughfare, especially at peak commuting time, Mirium and team have done an impressive job of building up a loyal band of followers, knowing most of their regular customers' orders and having them brewed up before they even reach the counter.

INSIDER'S TIP GET BEARPIT SOCIAL CATERING FOR BREAKFAST, LUNCH AND AFTERNOON OFFICE FUNCTIONS TOO

'We've transformed The Bearpit with coffee and food made with love to bring people together,' she says.

Wogan coffee that's roasted in the city is accompanied by unique sandwich fillings, juices made with a masticating juicer and an ever-changing and very popular vegan and gluten-free lunch special that draws in customers on a daily basis. That and the cakes and pastries from some of Bristol's top-notch bakers, of course.

'It's our customers' relentless support and love that helps us get through the winter and the tough times of The Bearpit,' she beams.

KEY ROASTER
Wogan Coffee

BREWING METHODS
Espresso, filter

MACHINE
Astoria Plus 4 You

GRINDER
Fiorenzato F83E

OPENING HOURS
Mon-Fri 7am-4pm
Sat 9am-4pm

www.bearpitsocial.co.uk   T: 07754 349580

f Bearpit Social   @bearpitsocial

№30. TINCAN COFFEE CO.

234 North Street, Southville, Bristol, BS3 1JD.

Proudly serving up speciality coffee since 2011, many people will know and love Tincan for its roving vintage cafe vans that tour the festies.

However you don't need to hit the road to track them down anymore, as they've opened their first static pit stop on Bristol's funky North Street.

The house blend (courtesy of local roaster Clifton) plays the leading role in a line-up of supporting stars including single origin filters, guest espresso and dishes such as baked eggs with dukkah, spinach, tomatoes and sourdough from the new brunch menu.

INSIDER'S TIP CHECK OUT THE BESPOKE CITROEN VAN WALLPAPER IN THE LOOS, ESPECIALLY MADE FOR TINCAN

It's going so well that owners Adam and Jessie have plans to roll out a sister cafe per year going forward. Indeed, if they follow the neighbourhood feel of this Southville gaff, they'll be on the right track, as it has become a hub in the community and is filled with parents and kids, freelancers and Southville originals, all enjoying the friendly vibe.

KEY ROASTER
Clifton Coffee Roasters

BREWING METHODS
Espresso, bulk brew filter

MACHINE
Custom Linea PB

GRINDERS
Mythos One x 2, Compak

OPENING HOURS
Mon-Sat 8am-6pm
Sun 9am-5pm

WIFI

DISABLED ACCESS

---

www.tincancoffee.co.uk   T: 01179 633979

f Tincan Coffee Co.   @tincancoffeeco   @tincancoffeeco

NO. 31. TINCAN COFFEE CO. TRUCKS

Major music festivals and events across the South West and UK.

Tincan's vintage Citroen vans have been garnering love for over five years as they've trawled the best festivals, keeping coffee lovers perked up in sometimes testing conditions.

'We like to think we provide the best tasting, highly crafted specialist coffee in the field at festies and high profile sporting events,' says owner Adam White.

The fleet of 1960s and 70s vintage trucks have been lovingly restored and converted for cafe life on the road, with top-end espresso equipment to take the specialist coffee experience wherever it's required. It even did the honours at the launch of the inaugural *South West Indy Coffee Guide*.

INSIDER'S TIP: PUT IT ON THE BUCKET LIST: FLAT WHITE AND TINCAN SALTED CARAMEL BUBBLE BAR DEVOURED IN A FIELD

As with the new bricks and mortar establishment in Bristol's Southville, the vans serve up Tincan's own seasonal blend that's put together by Clifton Coffee Roasters – along with treats such as blueberry bakewells and dark 'n' fruity flapjacks.

KEY ROASTER
Clifton Coffee Roasters

BREWING METHOD
Espresso

MACHINE
La Spaziale S5

GRINDERS
Mazzers

OPENING HOURS
As per event

Gluten FREE

 SOYA MILK AVAILABLE

 OUTDOOR SEATING

 FAMILY FRIENDLY

www.tincanevents.co.uk/events   T: 07725 880581

Tincan Events   @tincanevents   @tincanevents

M 100 HD
Inspired by the Future

№32. BOSTON TEA PARTY
8 Alfred Street, Bath, BA1 2QU.

Bright, spacious and decorated with Colonial style inspo, it's no wonder that Boston Tea Party's new venue in Bath is up for a couple of national design awards this year.

Tucked away on a quiet street, and just a quick caffeine dash from the city centre, it has more space to spread out (so you can take time over your brew) than its sister cafe over on Kingsmead Square. The result is that the refurbished Grade II-listed building on Alfred Street is a great spot for lazy weekend brunches and happy lunches with kids in tow.

INSIDER'S TIP THE CHORIZO HASH WITH PORTOBELLO MUSHROOMS AND POACHED EGGS IS THE ONLY WAY TO START THE WEEKEND

Keeping up with Bath's thriving speciality scene, head barista Beth and gang offer a monthly filter coffee alongside the two house blends – medium and dark roast – from Bristol's Extract Coffee Roasters, keeping the top-notch food bill in good company. The team has been swotting up on tea too, with a speciality recommendation on the counter each month.

KEY ROASTER
Extract Coffe Roasters

BREWING METHODS
Espresso, Marco batch brew

MACHINE
La Marzocco Linea Classic

GRINDER
Mazzer Major

OPENING HOURS
Mon-Sat
7am-7pm
Sun 8am-6pm

 Gluten FREE

 COFFEE BEANS AVAILABLE

 SOYA MILK AVAILABLE

 WIFI

 CYCLE FRIENDLY

 OUTDOOR SEATING

 FAMILY FRIENDLY

 DISABLED ACCESS

 DOG FRIENDLY

www.bostonteaparty.co.uk   T: 01225 425318
f Boston Tea Party Cafés   🐦 @btpcafes   📷 @btpcafes

33. PICNIC COFFEE

9 Saracen Street, Bath, BA1 5BR.

Whether you're stopping by for a take-out en route to work, a long overdue catch up with friends, or attending one of the lively music nights, there's a brew for every occasion waiting at Bath's Picnic Coffee.

Owners Tim and Kate only stock the best speciality grade stuff, choosing beans with distinct flavour profiles and unique cup characteristics from a cluster of artisan roasters.

INSIDER'S TIP BRING YOUR CAFFEINE LOVING POOCH ALONG FOR THE RIDE, THIS PLACE IS SUPER DOGGY FRIENDLY

Pick Tim or barista Jenn's brains for the latest tasting notes and best serve style combinations, as the friendly duo could chat coffee all day.

A nice selection of travel books, cosy sofas and a couple of tables on the pavement mean you can stay awhile at this sociable hub, plus there's a good selection of homemade sandwiches and cakes if you stop off at snack time, too. Often open late on Fridays for Picnic Unplugged, take the opportunity to sample some local craft beers, a glass of wine or even an evening espresso with the band.

KEY ROASTER
Easy José

BREWING METHODS
Espresso, V60, AeroPress, cold brew

MACHINE
Victoria Arduino Black Eagle

GRINDERS
Mahlkonig K30, Mahlkonig Varios, Compak E8

OPENING HOURS
Mon-Fri
7.30am-6pm
Sat 8.30am-6pm
Sun 9am-6pm

www.picniccoffee.co.uk   T: 01225 330128
f Picnic Coffee   🐦 @picnic_bath   📷 @picnic_bath

№34. CASCARA

3 Upper Borough Walls, Bath, BA1 1RG.

With some of the country's biggest coffee guns residing in the city, there was always going to be serious competition launching a speciality coffee shop in Bath. But with years of cumulative experience behind the bar, a cosy spot close to the centre and some fresh coffee concepts, Jay and Ana always had more than a fighting chance of success.

INSIDER'S TIP LOOK OUT FOR JAY'S MINIMAL HOME BREWING MASTERCLASSES COMING SOON

Since opening in December 2015, barista Jay – who heads up the coffee side of the business – has been experimenting with a rotating line-up of roasters, from the hyper-local Round Hill Roastery to Iceland-inspired Sundlaug Coffee Co. And as the name suggests, Jay also has a soft spot for the husks of the coffee cherry, so visitors will find at least two cascara infusions to sample.

The super healthy, fruit 'n' veg packed juices – and their less angelic baked neighbours on the counter – are created by partner Ana, making sticking around to grab a spot in the comfy seating area (where shoes are entirely optional) very worth it.

KEY ROASTER
Round Hill Roastery

BREWING METHODS
Espresso,
AeroPress

MACHINE
La Marzocco
Linea PB

GRINDERS
Nuova Simonelli
Mythos One,
Mahlkonig EK43

OPENING HOURS
Mon-Fri 9am-6pm
Sat 10am-6pm
Sun 10am-5.30pm

T: 07415 127774
f Cascara Bath   🐦 @cascarabath   📷 @cascarabath

35. SOCIETY CAFE

19 High Street, Bath, BA1 5AJ.

The younger, slicker and more energetic of the two Bath venues, Society Cafe's set-up at The Corridor is your go-to for an insanely good brew on-the-go.

Sitting pretty in a swish glass fronted building on the city's High Street, there's not a lot of space at this Scandi-inspired coffee shop. With just a handful of stools up top and 15 seats downstairs - you'll be fighting the local workforce for a window spot. That said, the limited seating shouldn't deter as there is some seriously good coffee to be savoured en-route to your next destination.

INSIDER'S TIP SNOOP OUT SOCIETY'S NEW DIGS IN OXFORD NEXT TIME YOU'RE IN THE CITY

Keeping things fresh, the house roaster has been switched up, with Cornwall's Origin now stocking the two grinders with its latest haul. Round Hill Roastery's fans shouldn't sweat though, as the local roaster still makes regular appearances, alongside an impressive line-up of guest roasters which changes by the week.

There's also a tempting selection of pastries and cakes from The Bertinet Bakery, and Made by Ben's toasties and sandwiches for appetites as active as your schedule.

KEY ROASTER
Origin Coffee

BREWING METHODS
Espresso,
AeroPress,
Clever dripper

MACHINE
La Marzocco
Linea PB

GRINDERS
Mahlkonig K30
Twin Vario,
Mahlkonig EK43

OPENING HOURS
Mon-Sat
7.30am-6pm
Sun 9am-6pm

www.society-cafe.com   T: 01225 428008

f Society Cafe   @societycafe   @societycafe

№36. JACOB'S COFFEE HOUSE

6 Abbey Churchyard, Bath, BA1 1LY.

One of Bath's original independent speciality spots, Jacob's Coffee House has earned a firm following of coffee buffs and caffeine tourists over the past five years.

Grinding the beans for every cup to order, stocking the freshest beans (from sister venue Mokoko, Easy José and guest roasters), and assembling the team for monthly cupping sessions to determine the next haul are a few of the ways that owner Jake Harris keeps 'em coming back for more.

INSIDER'S TIP EATING CLEAN? CHECK OUT THE RAW CACAO AND CHIA VEGAN CAKE

We reckon the fabulous rotating guest filters on the Marco Jet, locally sourced lunches (panini, soups and pies – you know the drill) and cakes from the in-house pastry chef have a part to play in the loyal legacy too.

With a beautiful venue nestled between Bath Abbey and The Pump Rooms, this is the kind of place where you'll want to stick around and soak up the surroundings. Grab one of the leather sofas upstairs or a table outside if you've got half an hour to spare.

KEY ROASTERS
Mokoko, Easy José

BREWING METHODS
Espresso,
Marco Jet filter

MACHINE
Conti Monte Carlo

GRINDERS
Mahlkonig K30
Air x 3

OPENING HOURS
Mon-Sun
8am-6pm

www.jacobscoffeehouse.com   T: 01225 758132

Jacob's Coffee House   @jacobscoffeehse   @jacobscoffeehse

37. COLONNA & SMALL'S

6 Chapel Row, Bath, BA1 1HN.

There are a number of reasons why Bath has become a mecca for coffee worshipers, although Colonna & Small's presence in the city is probably the one cementing its status.

Its modest shop front doesn't reveal much about the speciality sorcery going down inside the contemporary space. However, the stack of trophies belonging to co-owner, and triple UK Barista Champ, Maxwell Colonna-Dashwood, suggest something unusual is going on here.

Once inside, the passion for and knowledge of coffee quickly becomes clear. An impressive menu of seasonally-led espresso and filter based drinks have only got better this year with the introduction of beans roasted at Colonna's own roastery.

INSIDER'S TIP
THE RANGE OF COLONNA'S OWN ROASTED COFFEES WILL SOON BE AVAILABLE IN CAPSULES

Divided into three genres – Foundation, Discovery and Rare – and changing depending on seasonality and lot size of the bean, Colonna brings some of the world's rarest and most sought-after coffees to the commercial and domestic table.

Ask one of the savvy baristas to guide you through the intriguing flavour notes and preferred serve styles, then savour what could quite possibly be the best coffee you've ever tasted.

KEY ROASTER
Colonna

BREWING METHODS
Espresso, lungo
AeroPress, syphon,
Clever dripper
with V60 papers

MACHINE
Sanremo Opera

GRINDER
Mahlkonig EK43

OPENING HOURS
Mon-Fri
8am-5.30pm
Sat 8.30am-5.30pm
Sun 10am-4pm

www.colonnaandsmalls.co.uk   T: 07766 808067

Colonna and Small's   @colonna_smalls   @colonnacoffee

38. THE BATH COFFEE COMPANY

14 Kingsmead Square, Bath, BA1 2AD.

The cafe counterpart to the city's Square Root Coffee Roastery, The Bath Coffee Company is the speciality spot in which to get your hands on a freshly brewed cup of the roaster's beany bounty.

Housed in one of the grand old buildings on Kingsmead Square, there's plenty of space, inside and out, in which to take time over an expertly prepared espresso based brew or a filter from the single origin selection.

Small batch roasts of seasonal offerings mean there's usually something new to try, and with owner and master roaster, Adrian Smith, often pulling shots behind the bar, there's no one better to ask for the tasting notes.

INSIDER'S TIP: PICK UP A BAG OF SQUARE ROOT'S SUPERB 'THE SOLUTION' BLEND IN-STORE

A tempting array of daily specials, cakes and pastries to take-away keep the busy mix of tourists and locals fuelled for a day in the city. Or, if you've got some time to spare, grab a board game and challenge your fellow coffee connoisseurs to a Cluedo contest.

KEY ROASTER
Square Root
Coffee Roastery

BREWING METHODS
Espresso,
AeroPress

MACHINE
La Pavoni

GRINDER
Francino
La Pavoni

OPENING HOURS
Mon-Sun 8am-6pm

 Gluten FREE

 COFFEE BEANS AVAILABLE

 SOYA MILK AVAILABLE

 WIFI

 CYCLE FRIENDLY

 OUTDOOR SEATING

 COFFEE COURSES AVAILABLE

 FAMILY FRIENDLY

 DISABLED ACCESS

DOG FRIENDLY

www.bathcoffeecompany.co.uk   T: 01225 314881

f The Bath Coffee Company   🐦 @thebathcoffeeco

39. SOCIETY CAFE

5 Kingsmead Square, Bath, BA1 2AB.

As a firm favourite with Bath's foodie fraternity, it's not just coffee buffs that you'll find frequenting this Kingmead Square hangout, but pram-laden mums catching up over flat whites, students with heads buried in books on their third espresso and foodies snapping piccolos for their Twitter feed.

There's a passion for specialty coffee to be found at this modern and spacious cafe, with a keen team of SCAE trained baristas cranking out delicious coffee, courtesy of house roaster Origin. *'It's all about making our customers feel comfortable,'* explains barista Vicky. *'Stopping by a cafe, even if it's just for a five minute break, is a treat. We don't want to force the speciality spiel on our regulars but if people want to learn, we're happy to chat coffee.'*

INSIDER'S TIP
LOOK OUT FOR SOCIETY CAFE'S NEW PAD IN BRISTOL WHICH OPENS SOON

Customers are invited to join in with the guys' monthly cupping sessions, and you can always ask the friendly crew what's new on guest and filter. There's a rotating gang of bakers supplying the afternoon indulgences, so a slice of carrot cake or a doorstop sarnie is warranted for research purposes.

KEY ROASTER
Origin Coffee

BREWING METHODS
Espresso,
AeroPress,
cold brew

MACHINE
La Marzocco
Linea PB

GRINDERS
Mahlkonig EK43,
Mahlkonig
Tanzania, Nuova
Simonelli Mythos

OPENING HOURS
Mon-Fri
7am-6.30pm
Sat 7.30am-6.30pm
Sun 9am-6pm

Gluten FREE

COFFEE BEANS AVAILABLE

SOYA MILK AVAILABLE

WIFI

CYCLE FRIENDLY

OUTDOOR seating

FAMILY friendly

www.society-cafe.com T: 01225 442433

f Society Cafe   @societycafe   @societycafe

NO. 40. MOKOKO

7 Dorchester Street, Southgate, Bath, Somerset, BA1 1SS.

Conveniently located opposite Bath train station, Mokoko should be your first port of call on a caffeinated voyage around the historic city.

What it lacks in size, it certainly makes up for in variety, with a well-equipped brew bar and a choice of at least three different beans – including its own Mokoko roast – for coffee dudes to deliberate over. If it's busy (of course it's busy) grab a cup to-go en route to your next location, or if you find a moment of quiet (lucky you), pull up one of the stools in the window and pair your pick with one of the cakes from Mokoko's Bristol bakery.

INSIDER'S TIP
STOCK UP ON EQUIPMENT FOR THE HOME BREW BAR WITH FRIENDLY ADVICE FROM THE CREW

Standing proudly as an independent among a deluge of city centre chains, Mokoko's continued to see off competition from corporate competitors this year, introducing even more guest roasters from around the world and a new line-up of concoctions such as tonics, cascara and hibiscus to the menu.

KEY ROASTERS
Gardelli, La Cabra, Easy José

BREWING METHODS
Espresso, V60, AeroPress, Chemex, Kalita

MACHINE
Conti Monti Carlo

GRINDERS
Mahlkonig Vario K30 Tanzania, EK43

OPENING HOURS
Mon-Sun
7.30am-6.30pm

Gluten FREE

COFFEE BEANS AVAILABLE

SOYA MILK AVAILABLE

WIFI

CYCLE FRIENDLY

OUTDOOR SEATING

DOG FRIENDLY

www.mokokocoffee.com T: 01225 333444

f Mokoko @mokokocoffee @mokokocoffee

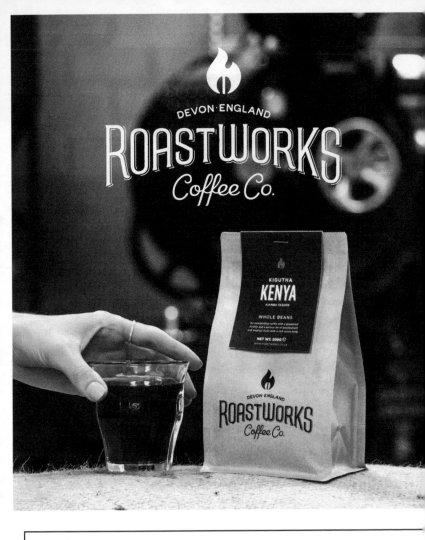

ARTISAN COFFEE ROASTED IN DEVON

WE'RE AN INDEPENDENT SPECIALITY COFFEE ROASTER DEDICATED TO ENGAGIN
CAFES AND CONSUMERS IN BETTER COFFEE. YOU CAN NOW BUY OUR COFFEES
INCLUDING OUR STUNNING NEW RANGE OF NESPRESSO® COMPATIBLE CAPSULE
THROUGH OUR WEBSITE - ROASTWORKS.CO.UK

INSTAGRAM.COM/ROASTWORKS_COFFEE_CO
@ROASTWORKSDEVON
FB.COM/ROASTWORKSCOFFEECO
ROASTWORKS.CO.UK

41. THE RIVER HOUSE

7 The Bridge, Frome, Somerset, BA11 1AR.

You won't find many places where the baristas scribble love letters in latte art and sneak a cheeky shot into your coffee (on request, of course), but that's how things roll at The River House in Frome.

The love child of owner Ellen Porteous' passion for fabulous food and affection for the rolling hills of her hometown, this funky cafe-come-bar-come-generally-cool-place-to-hang-out not only cranks out badass brunches and cracking cocktails but also stonking cups of Dusty Ape coffee.

INSIDER'S TIP CHECK OUT THE EVENING MENU OF SMALL PLATES FROM 6PM

Whether you go classic espresso or experiment with the AeroPress, you're in for an expertly prepared cup from coffee-obsessed barista Olly (with a rosetta tat on his forearm, dedication to the brew or what?)

From the bean blend to the decor, things don't stick around for long here, so when you spot something tasty on the Mexican inspired brunch menu – the smoky potato hash and sweetcorn fritters with grilled halloumi are good – make sure to ask the friendly staff for the recipe.

KEY ROASTER
Dusty Ape

BREWING METHODS
Espresso,
AeroPress

MACHINE
Astoria Plus

GRINDER
Cimbali Magnum
Macap MXDL

OPENING HOURS
Mon 8am-5pm
Tue-Fri 8am-11pm
Sat 9am-11pm
Sun 10am-4pm

www.riverhousefrome.co.uk   T: 01373 464847

f The River House   🐦 @riverhousefrome   📷 @riverhousefrome

42. STRANGERS WITH COFFEE

31 St Cuthbert Street, Wells, Somerset, BA5 2AW.

One for the curious coffee connoisseur, there's nearly always something new to try at this charming little coffee shop in Somerset's smallest city.

With caffeine fanatic Ivan Hewitt at the helm, visitors will find an ever-evolving menu of house blends and exciting guest roasts alongside a comprehensive brew bar from which to sample the latest find. *'We've introduced some new guest roasts this year,'* says Ivan, *'Colonna in Bath's geisha has been an absolute hit on filter, and regulars are always keen to catch up with our latest finds.'*

INSIDER'S TIP FEATURED IN THE LATEST EDITION OF THE LONELY PLANET GUIDE, IVAN AND SUSAN HAVE HAD VISITORS FROM AS FAR AS AUSTRALIA SEEKING THEM OUT

Susan heads up the foodie offering, with a solid bill of Mediterranean inspired dishes to keep caffeine tourists fuelled for onward travels. From the falafel in the wraps, to the sky-high cakes and the chutney oozing out of the cheese sarnies, everything is homemade and locally sourced, with pleasing options for veggies, vegans and dairy dodgers too.

KEY ROASTER
Allpress Espresso

BREWING METHODS
Espresso, V60, pourover, syphon, AeroPress, cold brew

MACHINE
La Marzocco Linea

GRINDERS
Mazzer Kony, Super Jolly Vario

OPENING HOURS
Tues-Sat
7.30am-4pm

 Gluten FREE

 COFFEE BEANS AVAILABLE

 SOYA MILK AVAILABLE

 CYCLE FRIENDLY

 OUTDOOR SEATING

 COFFEE COURSES AVAILABLE

 FAMILY FRIENDLY

 DOG FRIENDLY

T: 07728 047233

f Strangers With Coffee

№43. YEO VALLEY HQ

Rhodyate, Blagdon, Bristol, BS40 7YE.

There are few speciality joints that can rival the views that go with a morning cup at Yeo Valley HQ in Blagdon.

Perched on the edge of the Mendip Hills, overlooking the lush valleys below, this staff canteen turned foodie destination is the perfect place to savour a good brew away from the hustle and bustle of the city.

A stone's throw from Bristol Airport, the local, organic and seasonal food served at the family farm's quirky headquarters was such a hit with the staff that they've let everyone else in on the edible action and opened the doors to the public for breakfast, lunch and pop-up dinners.

INSIDER'S TIP LOOK FOR THE COWS GRAZING BY THE LAKE FROM THE FLOOR TO CEILING WINDOWS

With such high foodie standards, only the best coffee beans would do, and that's taken care of by Bristol roasters Extract. Sample the house blend on espresso, filter and french press with fresh milk from the farm. For a real treat, go for a shot pulled over Yeo Valley's own luxury vanilla ice cream.

KEY ROASTER
Extract Coffee Roasters

BREWING METHODS
Espresso, filter, french press

MACHINE
S5 Compact ED Group 2

GRINDER
Mazzer Lux

OPENING HOURS
Mon-Fri
9am-4pm
(booking essential for lunch)

www.yeovalleyvenues.co.uk   T: 01761 462798

f Yeo Valley   🐦 @yeovalley   📷 @ yeovalley

44. CALM COFFEE BAR

62 High Street, Burnham-on-sea, Somerset, TA8 1PE.

No need for post-glut guilt after a quick coffee escalates into two flat whites, lunch and a slice of cake at this gourmet coffee shop, 'cause if it's not organic, ethically sourced and nutritiously delicious, it's not on the menu at Burnham-on-Sea's Calm Coffee Bar.

Two top-quality espresso blends from local roaster Extract accompany the inventive veggie boxes, toasted panini and gluten-free bakes at this laid-back venue. Try the organic and house espressos, black for full flavour, white with Yeo Valley's organic milk, or whizzed up in a shake with chocolate whey protein, milk and crushed ice for ultimate #gains.

INSIDER'S TIP DO YOUR BIT FOR THE ENVIRONMENT WITH CALM'S REFILL FRIDAY CAMPAIGN

If you do feel the need to "exercise" your edible sins, follow the spiral staircase up to the Calm Studio where owner Tiffany and team hold personal training sessions, yoga and Pilates classes. It's not just the natural food and workout that'll make you feel good either, as the coffee bar's profits go to charity, FrankWater.

KEY ROASTER
Extract Coffee Roasters

BREWING METHOD
Espresso

MACHINE
La Marzocco

GRINDER
Mahlkonig K30

OPENING HOURS
Mon-Sat 8am-5pm
Sun 9am-3pm

www.calmcoffeebar.com

f Calm   🐦 @calmcoffeebar   📷 @calmcoffeebar

45. FINCA

11 High Street, Yeovil, Somerset, BA20 1RG.

This is the second speciality spot from the team who brought nitro cold brew, 90+ SCAA coffees and all other manner of caffeine wizardry to Dorchester. Yep, Finca has just bumped Yeovil up a number of places in the coffee tour rankings.

Opened in July 2016, the town centre venue provides a modern space – all chipboard, bare wood and stainless steel – in which to luxuriate in some of the finest coffees in a variety of exciting and creative serve styles.

INSIDER'S TIP STOCK UP ON HOME-ROASTED BEANS TO TAKE HOME

Like its sister venue (also named after the Spanish term for "estate"), all of the beans ground and brewed here are hand roasted on the small batch roaster at its Dorchester shop, with only the very best greens making the grade. Finca constantly cups various coffee samples ensuring that it delivers exciting and changing coffees throughout the year.

Its sibling also provides the toasted sandwiches and homemade cakes available to calm any coffee shakes after sampling a little too much of the new, seasonal cold brew.

KEY ROASTER
Finca

BREWING METHODS
Espresso,
AeroPress,
cold brew,
V60

MACHINE
La Marzocco

GRINDERS
Olympus, Mazzer

OPENING HOURS
Tue-Sat 8am-4pm

www.fincacoffee.co.uk

f Finca Yeovil 🐦 @scouting4coffee 📷 @scouting4coffee

WILTSHIRE
& DORSET

46. LEYKERS COFFEE CENTRAL

1 White Hart Yard, Trowbridge, Wiltshire, BA14 8BY.

With a whopping 75 years of experience between them, the team of baristas pulling shots and perfecting latte art at Leykers Coffee Central certainly know their filter from their flat white.

Inspired by a trip to Boston, Tracy and Graham Parker founded Trowbridge's first speciality spot way back when in 1999. Seventeen years on, the cosy corner cafe has seen off competition from a number of corporate competitors and continues to fly the flag for speciality brew – gaining a band of loyal locals along the way.

INSIDER'S TIP THERE'S OVER 30 FLAVOURS OF MILKSHAKE TO CHOOSE FROM

Plans for a refit in January 2017 see an exciting opportunity for the duo to expand Leyker's coffee offering, meaning visitors will be able to sample the beans of choice from Dusty Ape – and a couple of rotating guest roasters – on the spanking new brew bar, as well as from the espresso machine.

Renovations will also include a complete kitchen revamp, with more locally sourced and homemade quiches, chunky soups and tasty baked treats for caffeine tourists packing an appetite.

KEY ROASTER
Dusty Ape

BREWING METHODS
Espresso, filter

MACHINE
La Marzocco
Linea PB

GRINDERS
K30, Anfim

OPENING HOURS
Mon-Fri
7am-5.30pm
Sat 7am-5pm
Sun 9am-4pm

www.leykerscoffeecentral.com   T: 01225 768844

f Leykers Coffee Central   🐦 @coffee_central

47. GREENGAGES COFFEE HOUSE AND RESTAURANT

31 Catherine Street, Salisbury, Wiltshire, SP1 2DQ.

It's all about the detail at Greengages. Because what looks like a regular, bustling town cafe is actually a serious coffee lover's find – and a hot spot for gluten-free and vegan gourmets.

Let's talk coffee first. Obsessive barista (in the very best way), Joe Belsey is living, breathing and serving top-notch coffee day in, day out. Having chosen the excellent Round Hill as the house roaster (and enjoying his new EK43 grinder), he's squeezing every last drop of perfectly extracted goodness from single origin beans sourced across the globe.

When we visited, beans from Finca San Francisco in Costa Rica were so lip smackingly good with their boozy, rum 'n' raisin meets marzipan flavours that we were dreaming of it for days. *'I also use non-homogenised milk,'* says Joe, *'as I think it provides the very best flavour and texture'.*

INSIDER'S TIP BARISTA JOE CAME THIRD IN LAST YEAR'S INDY COFFEE GUIDE LATTE THROWDOWN

Plonk yourself on the coffee-sack covered bar in the window and chat to Joe as he crafts the coffee, or find a table on one of two floors and settle in for a bit of lunch. This is where the gluten-free goodies come into their own. The fish and chips is very popular, and at least half of the myriad of home-baked cakes are also gluten-free – and many vegan too. Almond and soy milk are also available.

KEY ROASTER
Round Hill Roastery

BREWING METHODS
Espresso, V60, AeroPress, Clever dripper, filter

MACHINE
La Marzocco Linea

GRINDER
EK43

OPENING HOURS
Mon-Fri
8am-5pm
Sat 8am-5pm

www.greengagessalisbury.co.uk T 01722 349934
f Greengages Coffeehouse & Restaurant @greengagescoffeehouse

48. BOSCANOVA

650 Christchurch Road, Boscombe, Bournemouth, Dorset, BH1 4BP.

The team roast, drink and love coffee at Boscanova - and the great thing is that they want to share it with their customers.

With global tunes pumping and a joyful jumble of caffeine-themed fixtures and fittings, such as the Lothair Harmann coffee cup lights and the "I love coffee" graffitied chair, it's easy to see why customers adore this inviting, eclectic and slightly eccentric cafe.

INSIDER'S TIP: DROP IN FOR THE HANG 10 BLEND FROM SISTER ROASTERY SOUTH COAST ROAST

Coming to a mug near you are single origin beans and blends, all freshly roasted by Heather Anderson on the premises or at sister cafe South Coast Roast.

Head chef Jim Hayward has been attracting a flurry of new customers to this eco-friendly stalwart of the speciality coffee scene, with his appealing menu of ever-changing mezze, specials, soups and brekkie feasts. And don't forget to check out his popular tartines at South Coast Roast too.

KEY ROASTER
South Coast Roast

BREWING METHODS
Espresso, drip filter

MACHINE
La Marzocco
2 group PID

GRINDERS
Mazzer, Anfim

OPENING HOURS
Mon-Fri 8am-4pm
Sat 8am-5pm
Sun 9am-4pm

www.thecaffeinehustler.com   T: 01202 242831

f Cafe Boscanova   @ @cafeboscanova

49. ESPRESSO KITCHEN

69 Commercial Road, The Triangle, Bournemouth, Dorset, BH2 5RT.

Whether it's zhooshing up a zany cheesegrater light or turning a retro telephone into an object d'art, Francesca Silvestre's background in costuming and design lends plenty of quirky personality to her cosy Bournemouth cafe.

INSIDER'S TIP THE CARROT CAKE IS PACKED FULL OF SPICY GINGER, CINNAMON AND NUTMEG GOODNESS

Surf boards suspended from the ceiling and vintage newspapers adorning the walls all add to the general kookiness of this coffee shop which attracts health-conscious regulars. Plus, of course, those desiring a seriously good espresso from a variety of top roasters.

In the heart of The Triangle, it's where the eco-conscious congregate in the knowledge that even the take-away cups are biodegradable.

This year, Francesca has opened an upstairs hidey-hole complete with fairy lights, colouring books, wooden tables and big windows. With something of an urban tree-house feel, it's an excellent vantage point for people watching.

Yet all this fab decor is not just style over substance, as a lot of thought goes into the food and drink. The coffee is organic, the cakes are homemade and organic and there are plenty of raw vegan and gluten-free options, too.

KEY ROASTER
Beanpress Coffee Company

BREWING METHOD
Espresso

MACHINE
La Marzocco FB70

GRINDERS
Mazzer Super Jolly x 2

OPENING HOURS
Mon-Sat 7am-7pm
Sun 10am-6pm

www.espressokitchen.co.uk   T: 01202 972420

f Espresso Kitchen Bournemouth   @expressokitchen   @espressokitchen

№50. COFFEE SALOON

9 Haven Road, Canford Cliffs, Poole, Dorset, BH13 7LE.

Donning a pair of Cuban heels and rocking up on horseback isn't compulsory if you are heading to one of the Coffee Saloons (although it may be encouraged), but a thirst for some of the best speciality brew around is certainly essential.

A stable of enthusiastic baristas behind the bar eagerly awaits caffeine-hungry travellers at this Deep South inspired hangout. Armed with a handpicked seasonal blend from Cornwall's Origin Coffee, some slick barista skills and acute attention to detail, their mission is to create a darn good cup every time.

INSIDER'S TIP THE AVO ON TOAST TASTES AS STUNNING AS IT LOOKS

The crew in the kitchen are putting just as much passion into the food served in the quirky, up-cycled joint, with Western flavours dominating the dishes. Whether you're a salt beef toastie kinda guy or a feta, spinach and sundried tomato muffin gal, make sure to pick up a slab of chocolate brownie for the saunter home.

Oh, and swing by and say howdy at Coffee Saloon's sister venues in Wareham and Poole.

KEY ROASTER
Origin Coffee

BREWING METHOD
Espresso

MACHINE
La Marzocco
Linear PB5

GRINDER
Nuova Simonelli
Mythos

OPENING HOURS
Mon-Sat 8am-4pm
Sun 9am-3pm

 Gluten FREE

 COFFEE BEANS AVAILABLE

 SOYA MILK AVAILABLE

 WIFI

 CYCLE FRIENDLY

 OUTDOOR Seating

 COFFEE COURSES AVAILABLE

 FAMILY FRiendly

 DISABLED ACCESS

DOG FRIENDLY

www.coffeesaloon.com   T: 01929 552416

f Coffee Saloon   🐦 @coffeesaloon   📷 @coffeesaloon

Your beverage menu requires equipment that is consistently reliable and precise. **Choose Experience. Choose BUNN.**

Quality Since 1840

bunn.com | 📷 @bunnquality

51. FINCA

41 Great Western Road, Dorchester, Dorset, DT1 1UF.

From hand roasting green beans for flat whites to creating freshly made sourdough sandwiches and cakes every morning, Finca takes homemade to delicious new heights at its shop in Dorchester.

All of the single origins served at this serious coffee shop are roasted in-store and whittled down from a vast selection of green beans on the sample roaster, ensuring only the tastiest crops feature on the constantly evolving menu.

INSIDER'S TIP **FINCA'S JUST SECURED A BREWING LICENSE – LOOK OUT FOR COFFEE BEER IN 2017**

A sophisticated brew bar and espresso set-up means there are numerous ways to sample the latest yield, and with cold brew and nitro available in summer, there's no doubt you'll be making a return trip for the one that got away. When the shakes set in, get the guys behind the bar to grind a bag to order, so that the sampling can continue at home.

Heavenly bakes and toasted sandwiches fresh from the kitchen keep the coffee company, though choosing just one slice may be as complex as selecting from the drinks offerings.

KEY ROASTER
Finca

BREWING METHODS
Espresso, AeroPress, Syphon, nitro, cold brew, V60

MACHINE
La Marzocco

GRINDERS
Olympus, Mazzer

OPENING HOURS
Mon-Sat 9am-4pm
Sun 10am-1pm

www.fincacoffee.co.uk

f Finca Dorchester 🐦 @scouting4coffee 📷 @scouting4coffee

№52. SOULSHINE

76 South Street, Bridport, Dorset, DT6 3NN.

With gorgeous graffiti scribbled over the walls, a blackboard above the bar laden with luscious lunch options and a shelf spanning the wall stocked with indie magazines, you'd be forgiven for forgetting your original intentions at Soulshine Cafe.

Though it's the speciality coffee served at this community cafe in the heart of Bridport that really shouldn't be overlooked. Extract Coffee Roasters supplies Soulshine with a stonking house blend to be savoured on espresso, with roasters from all over the UK making guest appearances on the second grinder and AeroPress.

While you're flicking through the latest edition of *Caffeine* mag, pair your coffee with something tasty from the wholesome breakfast or lunch menus - there are feel-good smoothies and juices too if you're in need of a non-caffeinated kick.

INSIDER'S TIP
TRY ONE OF THE REGULARLY CHANGING INDIE CRAFT BEERS

A bright and sunny courtyard means plenty of space for little ones to play, and there are babyccinos and a creative kids menu for future foodies and coffee gurus in the making.

KEY ROASTER
Extract Coffee Roasters

BREWING METHODS
Espresso, AeroPress

MACHINE
Sanremo Verona TCS

GRINDERS
Mahlkonig K30
Vario Air,
Sanremo SR50

OPENING HOURS
Mon-Sat 9am-5pm
Sun 10am-4pm

www.soulshinecafe.co.uk T: 01308 422821

f Soulshine Cafe 🐦 @soulshinecafe 📷 @soulshinecafe

53. AMID GIANTS & IDOLS

59 Silver Street, Lyme Regis, Dorset, DT7 3HR.

There's a new era evolving at Lyme's much loved speciality coffee shop.

Steve and Elaine took over from previous owner Xanne in July 2016, in a quest for a lifestyle change and eager to embrace the world of speciality coffee. Both are avid coffee lovers and have been interested in the coffee industry for many years.

INSIDER'S TIP TRY THE COAST HOUSE ROAST ALONGSIDE OTHER LOCALLY ROASTED SPECIALITY BEANS

Although they'll still be serving their own specially roasted Coast blend and decaf coffee, roasting will now take place off-site. However, they are keen to offer a regular variety of single origin coffees, so have hooked up with top quality local roasteries, Exeter's Crankhouse and Somerset's Brazier Coffee, which will supply guest beans to the coffee shop.

Alongside, Steve and Elaine aim to inspire customers by introducing them to a variety of locally roasted beans, through meet-the-roaster evenings. *'It's a chance for people to try out different equipment, meet other coffee lovers and enjoy great coffee,'* says Steve.

KEY ROASTERS
Amid Giants & Idols, Crankhouse Coffee, Brazier Coffee Roasters

BREWING METHODS
Espresso, AeroPress, pourover, wood neck, V60

MACHINE
La Marzocco Linea

GRINDERS
Mazzer

OPENING HOURS
Mon-Sun
10am-4pm

T: 07779 794381

ℕº54. READS ROASTBOX

Limekiln Farm, Sherborne, Dorset, DT9 6PS and at events across the South West.

If you want to taste Reads Coffee served just as head roaster Giles and the team of the Sherborne based roastery like to drink it, then you won't do better than to track down its mobile roastbox.

The horsebox is a fitting vehicle for Reads, as its roastery is based in rural splendour on a Dorset working farm.

INSIDER'S TIP: BUY READS ROASTERY BEANS-TO-GO AT THE SAME TIME

Drawing on many years of experience (Giles was an early proponent of the quality coffee scene in the UK), Reads specialises in the traditional roasting of single estate arabica coffees and the creation of unique espresso blends.

With 14 different coffees to choose from – from lighter contemporary styles to dark roasted Italian style blends – there's plenty of choice to get you swishing your tail.

Look out for the Reads Roastbox, an original Rice pony trailer, at events in Dorset and beyond and get stuck into some good gluten-free nosebag while you're at it.

KEY ROASTER
Reads Coffee

BREWING METHODS
Espresso, drip, pourover

MACHINE
Gaggia

GRINDERS
Gaggia, Bunn

OPENING HOURS
Available on request

www.readscoffee.co.uk　T: 01935 481010

f Reads Coffee Roasters　🐦 @reads_coffee　📷 @readscoffeeroasters

IF IT'S SUMMERTIME,
BRING ON THE AFFOGATO!

DEVON

Kim Sayer

55. THE GLORIOUS ART HOUSE

120 Fore Street, Exeter, Devon, EX4 3JQ.

Mexico goes to the circus, by way of Baz Luhrmann's *Romeo and Juliet* at Exeter's Glorious Art House. A melting pot of emerald, hot yellow and cerise walls, wild artwork, circus sign-writing and a flying gold cherub create a winning clash of creativity at this friendly cafe.

Don't worry that it's style over substance, as the coffee is pretty good too. Voyager's Road Trip is the house roast, but guest coffees change regularly from the likes of Clifton and local roaster Crankhouse. Owner Derry and his team of baristas are reassuringly coffee-obsessed, while Derry's artist mum Rosy adds the interior design and textile sculptures.

INSIDER'S TIP: LOOK OUT FOR THE OCCASIONAL LIVE MUSIC NIGHTS

There's no kitchen here, so everything is prepared in front of you on the bar – hot soup, fresh baguettes and locally made cakes – and there are a few good nooks in which to enjoy them. Join the conversation downstairs, find a spot on the first floor or head to the secret, fairy-lit garden and before you leave, be sure to check out the local artwork on display in the top floor gallery.

KEY ROASTER
Voyager Coffee Roasters

BREWING METHODS
Espresso, V60, Chemex

MACHINE
Sanremo Verona TCS

GRINDER
Sanremo SR50

OPENING HOURS
Mon-Sat
8am-5.30pm
Sun 10am-4pm

www.theglorious.co.uk   T: 01392 490060

f The Glorious Art House   🐦 @gloriousexeter   📷 @thegloriousarthouse

№56. EXPLODING BAKERY

1b Central Station Buildings, Queen Street, Exeter, Devon, EX4 3SB.

Oli and the team at Exploding Bakery have long been the insiders' fave find for innovative baking with seriously good coffee in Exeter.

With stacks of chains in the city, it's been a case of converting commuters pouring out of Exeter Central, one silky flat white and crisply yielding croissant at a time.

Clearly it's a case of "job done", as nowadays you can barely get in the place, it's so busy. That's why this autumn it's doubling in size by exploding into the shop space next door. *'It'll give us much more room for the bakery, and the opportunity to be really innovative with special bakes, as well as getting into making bread,'* says Oli.

In the name of research, he's been eating his way around the bakeries and coffee shops of New York, so expect some innovative developments in the new gaff.

Beautifully crafted coffee continues to be a key element of the experience, with the house blend by Monmouth (*'a good balance for the sweeter cakes'*) supplemented by guest roasts. There's also a new focus on cold brew, *'as we've finally found one we really like.'*

KEY ROASTER
Monmouth Coffee

BREWING METHODS
Espresso, V60, AeroPress, cold brew

MACHINE
La Marzocco Linea

GRINDERS
Mythos One x 2, Mazzer Super Jolly

OPENING HOURS
Mon-Fri 8am-4pm
Sat 9am-4pm

Gluten FREE

COFFEE BEANS AVAILABLE

SOYA MILK AVAILABLE

WiFi

CYCLE FRIENDLY

OUTDOOR SEATING

DISABLED ACCESS

INSIDER'S TIP DO THE COLD BREW AND SALTED CARAMEL BROWNIE PAIRING

---

www.explodingbakery.com T: 01392 427900

f The Exploding Bakery   @explodingbakery   @explodingbakery

57. IVAN'S COFFEE

The Bike Shop, 29-31 Leat Street, Tiverton, Devon, EX16 5LG.

Ivan's swapped four wheels for two in the latest incarnation of his speciality coffee offering. Although he's still taking his funky mobile VW coffee van out to festivals, you'll now find him most days at Tiverton's Bike Shop, tinkering with gears and group heads in equal measure.

'We want to make Ivan's Coffee at The Bike Shop in Tiverton, a hangout for cyclists and coffee drinkers,' he says. 'Cycling has been a passion of mine for a number of years and the bike boom has seen things really take off. We get a lot of touring cyclists and social riders from clubs, and whether you're riding from Land's End to John O'Groats or just passing by, we are always pleased to see you.'

INSIDER'S TIP FUEL YOUR RIDE WITH A HOMEMADE 'BONKERS BAR' FILLED WITH CEREALS, SEEDS AND PEANUT BUTTER

So Ivan's fixing bikes one moment and pouring shots from the coffee machine in the corner, the next. The beans are from local roasters Crediton Coffee, Crankhouse Coffee and Exe Coffee Roasters, as he's keen to support Devon businesses wherever possible. To that end, the milk is sourced from a local dairy and brownies come courtesy of Mrs Gill's Tiverton bakery.

KEY ROASTERS
Crediton Coffee,
Crankhouse Coffee

BREWING METHODS
Espresso, pourover,
AeroPress,

MACHINE
Rocket Espresso
Giotto Evoluzione

GRINDER
Sanremo S70 Evo

OPENING HOURS
Mon-Fri
9.30am-5.30pm
Sat 9am-2pm

www.ivans-coffee.com   07796 128057

Ivans coffee   @ivanscoffee   @ivanscoffee

№ 58. CHARLIE FRIDAYS COFFEE SHOP

Church Steps, Lynton, Devon, EX35 3HY.

It's not easy to find speciality coffee on Exmoor, but if you venture across the rolling hills and moorland to the charmingly authentic little Victorian town of Lynton, and head for the church steps, you'll be glad you made the effort. Because this quirky cafe and coffee shop is a real find among a plethora of touristy tea rooms.

INSIDER'S TIP
LOCALS LOVE THE REGULAR CURRY NIGHTS AND MUSIC EVENTS

Owner Anna has shipped in Extract beans from Bristol for the espresso based coffee menu, along with the introduction of divine milkshakes, happy cafe food and a cool playlist.

Where the locals in-the-know go, Charlie Fridays may only be in its second year of trading, and rather hidden due to its semi subterranean setting, but having won the award of north Devon's Cafe of the Year 2015, it's not going to remain a secret for long.

KEY ROASTER
Extract Coffee Roasters

BREWING METHOD
Espresso

MACHINE
Iberital Junior

GRINDER
Mazzer

OPENING HOURS
Sat–Thu
10am-6pm
Fri 10am-late

Gluten FREE

COFFEE BEANS AVAILABLE

SOYA MILK AVAILABLE

WIFI

CYCLE FRIENDLY

FAMILY FRIENDLY

DOG FRIENDLY

www.charliefridays.co.uk T: 07544 123324

f Charlie Friday's Coffee Shop @charliefridays @charliefridays

ᴺᴼ59. LOVE FROM MARJORIE

28 St James Place, Ilfracombe, Devon, EX34 9BJ.

You don't have to sit on a plane for 23 hours to get an authentic Aussie coffee experience anymore, as quirky, Victorian Ilfracombe has it covered.

Crafting Origin coffee in antipodean style (read: short and exquisite), the purist approach of the team at Marj's sees it focusing on espresso, with the addition of a few choice treats to keep the energy levels up. Classic Melbourne banana bread is baked daily and accompanied by pastries as well as raw snacks made by Tales of a Wooden Spoon, just up the road.

INSIDER'S TIP WE LOVE THE PARED-BACK COOL 70S DECOR WITH AUTHENTIC RETRO FITTINGS

Keeley and husband Andy launched the specialist coffee shop a year ago and have now returned Down Under, with brilliant barista Phoebe taking over the reins in their absence. Promising an uncompromising experience, with relentless attention to detail in-keeping with their Melbourne inspiration, Andy insists: *'we have a purist approach and are sticking to our guns – we won't serve huge lattes for example, just great coffee, food and choice cuts of music.'*

KEY ROASTER
Origin Coffee

BREWING METHOD
Espresso

MACHINE
La Marzocco
Linea PB

GRINDER
Nuova Simonelli
Mythos

OPENING HOURS
Thu-Sun
9am-3pm

www.lovefrommarjorie.com

 Love From Marjorie x 🐦 @lovefrommarj 📷 @lovefrommarjorie

№60. WILD THYME CAFE

5 Caen Field Shopping Centre, Braunton, Devon, EX33 1EE.

This community cafe in surfy Braunton is the perfect spot to head for a post-surf brekkie.

Grab a space out front and soak up the Braunton vibe as dudes roll past on skateboards, and surf wagons pull up crammed with kids, boogie boards and wetsuits on the way to Saunton beach.

The large menu is full of goodies, and you can go simple with fresh fruit and yogurt or the whole hog with Mexican scrambled eggs and butchers sausages. There are lots of vegetarian and vegan options too.

INSIDER'S TIP LOOK OUT FOR THE OCCASIONAL THAI NIGHTS

Come lunchtime, check out the Wild Thyme chilli dog or spicy coconut dahl, and take advantage of the opportunity to feed the kids interesting food off the main menu – just in mini portions.

The coffee is all espresso based, with Origin Coffee as the house blend and guest roasts appearing from the likes of Clifton Coffee. *'We've got a big group of regulars, so we like having guest roasts to give them something new to try,'* says owner Vicky.

KEY ROASTER
Origin Coffee

BREWING METHOD
Espresso

MACHINE
Astoria Plus 4 You

GRINDER
Mazzer Super Jolly Timer

OPENING HOURS
Mon-Sun 9am-4pm
Extended during summer

www.wildthymecafe.co.uk T 01271 815191
f Wild Thyme Cafe 🐦 @wildthymecafe 📷 @wildthymecafe

№61. BEATSWORKIN

6 Queen's House. Queen's Street, Barnstaple, EX32 8HJ.

When it comes to the grind – and we're talking both skateboard tricks and quality coffee – there are few as passionate as Glenn Field.

His caffeinated skate shop in Barnstaple – all poured concrete, exposed brickwork and walls showcasing stunning skateboards – is a homage to both.

When it came to choosing a main roaster for this coffee den, there was no contest for Glenn, who had already been serving organic Beanberry coffee at the back of his urban streetwear shop, two doors down.

INSIDER'S TIP **TIME TO SPARE? ORDER A V60 AND GRAB ONE OF THE BEAUTIFUL SKATE MAGS AND A SEAT IN THE WINDOW**

'To do the coffee wholeheartedly I wanted to use a speciality coffee roaster rooted in organic principles,' says Glenn, who is a trailblazer for sustainable living, and uses only biodegradable, organic packaging.

Drop by and hang out with the cool kids while fuelling up on wholesome cakes, oat and raw chocolate bars, nuts, organic energy drinks and smoothies made with hemp, spirulina and baobab.

KEY ROASTER
Beanberry

BREWING METHODS
Espresso, V60, Chemex

MACHINE
Sanremo Verona TCS

GRINDER
San Remo

OPENING HOURS
Mon-Sat 9am-6pm
Sun 11am-4pm

T 01271 321111

f Coffeenskate 🐦 @Beatsworkinuk 📷 @Beatsworkin

№62. THE ALMOND THIEF

Unit 3-4 Shinners Bridge Workshops, Webbers Way, Dartington, Devon, TQ9 6JY.

O ne rain-lashed winter in Wales, while waiting for his son to be born, Dan Mifsud decided to experiment with a spot of bread making. Armed with a cast iron pot and a sourdough recipe, he kept himself busy by baking on the Rayburn.

Then, just over a year ago (and many loaves later), the evolutionary biologist turned artisan baker opened The Almond Thief.

INSIDER'S TIP **TRY THE SABIH, AN IRAQI FAVOURITE WITH AUBERGINES, EGG AND GREEN CHILLI SAUCE**

Attracting laptop lingerers, coffee connoisseurs and bread heads, Dan's unassuming warehouse-style cafe on Dartington's industrial estate is a true hidden gem on the Devon coffee scene.

Grab a spot on a sharing bench and fritter away the day over a sticky, spicy brioche and Origin espresso, or a Crankhouse filter after your Middle Eastern style lunch.

The open-plan kitchen of the cafe bakery, also make it a great place to watch dextrous hands shaping dough into baguettes, fruit breads and sprouted loaves, all bound for local cafes, restaurants and shops.

KEY ROASTER
Origin Coffee

BREWING METHODS
Espresso, V60

MACHINE
Linea PB

GRINDERS
EK43, Mythos One

OPENING HOURS
Tues-Fri 8am-3pm
Sat 9am-1pm

www.thealmondthief.com T: 01803 411290

f The Almond Thief @thealmondthief @thealmondthief

63. CALYPSO COFFEE COMPANY

45 Fleet Street, Torquay, Devon, TQ2 5DW.

With its hand-crafted industrial-style chandeliers and copper piping, this spacious urban chic cafe on Torquay's busy Fleet Street offers everything – from espresso to cold brew – for those seeking a serious caffeine hit.

Owners Lucas and Lana also like to tempt customers with their unique homemade drinks, created from scratch using closely-guarded secret recipes.

INSIDER'S TIP — LOOK OUT FOR REGULAR CHARITY NIGHTS AT THIS COMMUNITY CAFE

Flavoured sugars are crafted into frothy delights – think sumptuous lavender or citrus cream coffees. While fruits, spices and seasoning are turned into exciting home brewed teas. And the innovation doesn't stop there: 'if someone comes up with a funky drink, we'll give it a go,' says Lucas.

Throw in traditional teas, cold coffees, real fruit smoothies, American style milkshakes and seasonal drinks and it's easy to see what makes Calypso, with its outside seating, a hit with those wanting to dawdle over breakfasts, bagels and freshly baked croissants.

KEY ROASTER
Square Mile
Coffee Roasters

BREWING METHODS
Espresso, V60,
AeroPress,
cold brew

MACHINE
La Marzocco
Linea 3 AV

GRINDERS
Mazzer Kony
Electronic,
Mahlkonig Tanzania

OPENING HOURS
Mon-Sat 8am-6pm
Sun 9am-6pm
Extended during
summer

 Gluten FREE

 COFFEE BEANS AVAILABLE

 SOYA MILK AVAILABLE

 WIFI

 CYCLE FRIENDLY

 OUTDOOR SEATING

 FAMILY FRIENDLY

 DISABLED ACCESS

DOG FRIENDLY

T: 01803 213728

Calypso Coffee Company   @calypso_coffee

Coffee Consultancy and Education

From barista basic and intermediate training;
to sensory, brewing and latte art workshops.
Coffea Arabica offers an understanding of coffee quality.

Visit our website for further information on our courses
www.coffeaarabica.co.uk

64. BAYARDS COVE INN

27 Lower Street, Dartmouth, Devon, TQ6 9AN.

Bayards Cove Inn is a definite must-visit in foodie Dartmouth, even with all the competition in town. A boutique townhouse hotel with cafe, coffee shop and restaurant on the ground floor, it's all wrapped up in the historic charm of a 14th century building.

INSIDER'S TIP: BAG YOURSELF A COSY SPOT ON ONE OF THE LEATHER SOFAS AND TAKE A WELL EARNED BREATHER FROM THE BUSY THRONG

You don't have to stay the night in order to visit, although homemade churros and chocolate for breakfast with an espresso on the side would certainly be a big enough draw.

Barista Callum Woodman takes care of the coffee side of things, working with Origin which provides the beans and trains the staff to get the best out of them. Pair it with a lush homemade cake, a proper Devonshire tea of scones and cream, or stay for lunch and try one of the cafe's popular homemade burgers.

Four-legged friends are very welcome and well looked after, making this a perfect pit stop after one of the area's stunning coastal walks.

KEY ROASTER
Origin Coffee

BREWING METHOD
Espresso

MACHINE
Sanremo

GRINDER
Sanremo

OPENING HOURS
Mon-Sun
8am-10pm

WIFI

www.bayardscoveinn.co.uk | 01803 839278

Bayards Cove Inn   @bayardscoveinn

65. COASTERS COFFEE COMPANY

Unit 1, Abbots Quay, Prince of Wales Road, Kingsbridge, Devon, TQ7 1DY.

There's an easy-going, throw-away-the-timetable vibe at this airy, modern cafe with its welcoming staff and mould-to-your-contours sofas. Tucked away in the charming market town of Kingsbridge, it's where locals go to spend a dilatory hour or two with friends, family, laptops and books.

INSIDER'S TIP A SPLIT SHOT (ESPRESSO & 4OZ MILK) IS PERFECT FOR THE INDECISIVE

At this vibrant meeting place, the house coffee is roasted by Clifton, alongside ever-changing espresso and filter menus, with guest roasts from the likes of Extract and Square Mile.

Popular all-day snacks include panini and sandwiches, plus bakes from Devon favourites Exploding Bakery and Peck & Strong.

Since opening in 2010, owners Jackie and Paul have attracted increasing numbers of tourists visiting the South Hams. With knowledgeable baristas, tasting notes on the blackboard and a range of beans and equipment to take home, it's now high on the hit list of many a visiting coffee-head.

KEY ROASTER
Clifton Coffee Roasters

BREWING METHODS
Espresso, Clever dripper, V60, AeroPress

MACHINE
La Marzocco Linea

GRINDERS
Nuova Simonelli Mythos One, Mahlkonig K30 Vario, Mazzer Super Jolly, Baratza Preciso

OPENING HOURS
Mon-Fri
8.30am-6pm
Sat 8.30am-5pm
Sun 9am-2pm

T: 01548 853004

 Coasters Coffee Company @coasterscoffee

№66. BOSTON TEA PARTY

Jamaica House, 82-84 Vauxhall Street, Sutton Harbour, Plymouth, Devon, PL4 0EX.

With retro up-cycled furniture, some seriously jazzy tiling and a design award on the mantelpiece, you'd never guess that Boston Tea Party's digs in Plymouth started out as a potato store.

Making the most of the three storey building, the Sutton Harbour venue has 150 seats inside – and an extra 30 outside – in which to sit back and relax with a good brew while enjoying the beautiful views over the marina.

After fuelling the caffeine addiction with one of Extract's house roasts or guest filters, hit your five-a-day with one of Boston's new raw veg smoothies. The Green One – spinach, cucumber, banana, chia seeds, apple juice and lime – was made for your Instagram feed (wedge of flapjack just out of shot).

INSIDER'S TIP
DARE TO TRY THE LATTE ART DICE. ROLL AND THE BARISTA WILL POUR THE DESIGN DECIDED BY FATE

Healthy goodies such as the brown rice porridge and smashed avo on toast feature in the foodie offering too, although the Big Boss brunch and Ambassador hazelnut cake are likely to throw all good intentions out of the window.

KEY ROASTER
Extract Coffee Roasters

BREWING METHODS
Espresso, batch brew

MACHINE
La Marzocco Linea Classic

GRINDER
Mazzer Major

OPENING HOURS
Mon-Sat
7am-7pm
Sun 8am-7pm

www.bostonteaparty.co.uk T: 01752 267862

Boston Tea Party Cafés   @btpcafes   @btpcafes

CORNWALL

GOOD VIBES CAFE
№ 69

P.116

67. LIBERTY COFFEE

4 Northgate Street, Launceston, Cornwall, PL15 8BD.

A veritable homage to the coffee bean, with its stripped back menu of single origin espressos and filters, Liberty Coffee is a place to tune up your palate.

And delighting in helping you discover global coffees is owner Ben Statton. Channelling precision and passion, this friendly bean maestro demonstrates just what can be achieved with a superb roast, skilled baristas and a thoroughly un-snobbish attitude to coffee.

INSIDER'S TIP THE SALTED CARAMEL BROWNIE IS A HOUSE BESTSELLER

'We don't want people to feel intimidated or stupid,' says Ben, whose education work includes a blog on his website, a coffee consultancy business, tasting events and brewing classes. 'Nor do we want people thinking coffee is just a cool thing for hipsters.'

It's attention to detail that pervades everything on offer at this welcoming community cafe, just off Launceston High Street. Whether that's roaster takeovers from the likes of Has Bean, daily fresh bakes, loose leaf single estate teas or the dazzling single origin Kokoa Collection hot chocolates.

KEY ROASTER
Multiple

BREWING METHODS
Espresso, AeroPress, cold brew, Clever dripper

MACHINE
La Marzocco Linea

GRINDER
Mythos One

OPENING HOURS
Mon-Sat
9am-5pm

www.liberty-coffee.co.uk   T 01566 773223

f Liberty Coffee   🐦 @libcoffee   📷 @libcoffee

№68. STRONG ADOLFOS

Hawksfield, A39, Wadebridge, Cornwall, PL27 7LR.

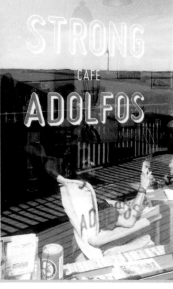

In an ideal world, every roadside pit stop would serve lip-smackingly good coffee and dreamy brunch dishes, but for now we'll settle with re-routing all of our trips via the Atlantic Highway for a top-notch brew and Scandi-inspired brekkie at Strong Adolfos.

Picking up the gong for Best Cafe at the *Food Magazine* Reader Awards 2016, owners John and Mathilda have created a winning mix of laid-back hospitality, lovely homemade food and, of course, some cracking coffee to fuel onward journeys.

Origin Coffee can be sampled on espresso, filter or Clever dripper. Then pair your poison with one of the delicious cakes from the bar and indulge in the Swedish tradition of fika – a snapshot at the cafe from Mathilda's homeland.

INSIDER'S TIP YOU'LL BE MAKING A RETURN TRIP TO SEE WHAT'S FRESH ON THE SPECIALS BOARD

Hungry road trippers are in for a treat, with an envy-inducing line-up of seasonal dishes coming from the kitchen. Try the Malayan fish curry, Thai beef salad, veggie scotch egg, and something sweet from the cake sideboard.

KEY ROASTER
Origin Coffee

BREWING METHODS
Espresso, Clever dripper, batch filter

MACHINE
La Marzocco

GRINDER
Nuova Simonelli

OPENING HOURS
Mon-Fri
8.30am-4.30pm
Sat 9am-5pm
Sun 9am-4.30pm

www.strongadolfos.com T: 01208 816949

Strong Adolfo's @strongadolfos @strongadolfos

69. GOOD VIBES CAFE

28 Killigrew Street, Falmouth, Cornwall, TR11 3PN.

'Flavour, colour and texture' is the rallying cry of Falmouth's Good Vibes Cafe; a motto that's apparent in everything from its funky decor to the original bakes.

Up-cycled furniture and colour-popping artwork bring a colourful irregularity to the setting, while a changing menu of breakfasts, bagels, sandwiches and specials score high on flavour.

INSIDER'S TIP TRY THE BACON OR HALLOUMI SIGNATURE SANDWICH PACKED WITH PAPRIKA HUMMUS, PICKLED ONIONS, GUACAMOLE AND TOMATO

Since taking over in May 2016, new owner and chef Dan Rossiter has been adding a few interesting twists of his own to the locally-sourced menu, while ensuring the cafe is still a hot spot for vegans and vegetarians seeking out inspiring meat-free dishes.

The coffee also reflects the cafe's motto with a seasonal blend from Cornish roasters Origin making for a tried-and-tested cup of goodness. 'We like to keep the coffee simple yet effective,' says Dan, 'by using a really consistent product that we know will be served at its best by our highly-trained baristas.'

KEY ROASTER
Origin Coffee

BREWING METHOD
Espresso

MACHINE
La Marzocco
Linea 3 group

GRINDERS
Malkonig K30 x 2

OPENING HOURS
Mon-Sat
8.30am-5pm
Sun 10am-2pm

www.goodvibescafe.tumblr.com T: 01326 211870

f Good Vibes Cafe   @good_vibes_cafe   @goodvibescafefalmouth

№70. PICNIC CORNWALL

14 Church Street, Falmouth, Cornwall, TR11 3DR.

For a true taste of Cornwall, Falmouth's welcoming, multi-award winning indie coffee shop takes some beating. Everything sold at Picnic Cornwall (which is also a deli and hamper service), is sourced within the county – and that includes the coffee.

Seasonal blends from Helston roasters Origin are freshly ground for each cup, often combined with local milk from Trewithen Dairy. It's a match made in coffee heaven according to owner Jo Foreman who makes sure that her staff get to visit all of Picnic's suppliers.

INSIDER'S TIP 'EAT, DRINK, EXPLORE,' SAYS PICNIC, SO GRAB A COFFEE AND SNACK AND HEAD OUTDOORS

'We have in-house coffee training from Origin but it's great for staff to actually visit the roastery and see the beans being roasted and understand their policies on sustainability,' she says.

In the summer, Jo and her team can be spotted just above Castle Beach, bringing coffee and Cornish fare to holidaymakers in the sea-green converted ambulance, Picnic Laurent. The van also makes appearances at local events and festivals.

KEY ROASTER
Origin Coffee

BREWING METHOD
Espresso

MACHINE
La Marzocco
FB80

GRINDER
Mazzer Luigi

OPENING HOURS
Mon- Sun
8.30am-5.30pm
Extended during
summer

www.picniccornwall.co.uk   T: 01326 211655

f Picnic Cornwall   🐦 @picniccornwall   📷 @picnic_cornwall

71. GYLLY BEACH CAFE

On Gyllyngvase Beach, Cliff Road, Falmouth, Cornwall, TR11 4PA.

For those who really do like to be beside the seaside, Gylly Beach Cafe, on Gyllyngvase's glorious stretch of silver sands is a must-visit. Because getting your chops around an espresso-based Origin coffee, while gazing over the azure waters is a pretty special experience.

The veranda seats are the most coveted spots where you can watch the paddlers, sun-seekers and dog walkers through the floor-to-sky windows. And in summer, this seaside hub, imbued with an award winning eco-friendly ethos by owners Simon and Viv Daw, holds open-air grills with jumbo hot dogs, venison burgers and a seafood bar packed with lobster and spider crab.

INSIDER'S TIP — THE BEACH-SIDE MUSIC NIGHTS ARE LEGENDARY

Whatever the season, new head chef Dale McIntosh sees to it that everyone leaves satisfied by the hearty Cornish breakfasts and ever-changing lunch and dinner dishes, all reflecting produce that's grown, reared and fished a stone's throw from the cafe.

KEY ROASTER
Origin Coffee

BREWING METHOD
Espresso

MACHINE
La Marzocco

GRINDER
Espresso Italiano

OPENING HOURS
Mon-Sun
9am-late

www.gyllybeach.com   T: 01326 312884

f Gylly Beach Cafe   🐦 @gyllybeachcafe   📷 @gyllybeachcafe

72. HUB ST IVES

4 Wharf Road, St Ives, Cornwall, TR26 1LF.

If the perfect seaside coffee haven exists, it could just be Hub St Ives. Grab a seat on the upstairs balcony for a vista of turquoise waters, cliffs packed with cute cottages, ocean-going boats and happy hordes of sun-seeking holidaymakers.

For big burgers, big views and speciality coffee that's big on taste, this is a great harbourside find.

INSIDER'S TIP: LOVE TALKING COFFEE? BARISTA MARCUS IS ALWAYS HAPPY TO CHAT BEANS AND BREW

Eye-wateringly generous burgers, like the award winning Big Kahuna, and American inspired snacks such as trays of barbecued pulled pork, are offered alongside Origin espresso and filter batch brews – the latter being a nifty way to cope with high-season demand for a great cup of coffee.

'It's comparable to a pourover but is a quicker, smarter way to keep up,' says barista Marcus, who used to be a roaster at Origin. *'With multiple orders and up to 10 coffees on each check, it ensures everyone gets a quality cup.'*

KEY ROASTER
Origin Coffee

BREWING METHODS
Espresso, batch brew

MACHINE
La Marzocco Strada

GRINDER
Nuova Simonelli Mythos One

OPENING HOURS
Mon-Sun
9am-late

www.hub-stives.co.uk   T: 01736 799099

Hub   @hubstives   @hubstives

MAP № 73. THE YELLOW CANARY CAFE
12 Fore Street, St Ives, Cornwall, TR26 1AB.

Y ou can grab and go, or take it slow, at this cosy cafe in the Cornish port famed for its lucid light, golden beaches and celebrated artists.

And should you find yourself unable to resist a freshly-baked pastel de nata oozing with creamy custard or a whopping sandwich loaded with locally-landed crab alongside your Origin-roasted house or seasonal espresso, who would blame you?

INSIDER'S TIP
LOAD UP ON CORNISH CLASSICS SUCH AS AWARD WINNING PASTIES AND GOOEY CREAM TEAS

Owners Paul and Ylenia Haase are up at the crack of dawn to bake moreish favourites, such as their maple syrup and Cornish butter laden flapjacks, appreciated as much by sit-in customers as those pausing at the hatch beneath the cheery yellow sign on Fore Street.

With a long history in the town – it was first established in 1972 – The Yellow Canary is a firm fave in St Ives, and worth putting on the hit list for visiting coffee lovers, so you can do coffee and biscotti in the mornings with the locals.

KEY ROASTER
Origin Coffee

BREWING METHODS
Espresso, AeroPress

MACHINE
La Marzocco Linea

GRINDER
Mazzer Major E

OPENING HOURS
Mon-Sun
March-November
Summer
7am-10pm
Winter
9am-5pm

 COFFEE BEANS AVAILABLE
 SOYA MILK AVAILABLE
 DOG FRIENDLY

www.theyellowcanary.com T: 01736 797118

 The Yellow Canary Cafe   @yellowcanarycaf   @theyellowcanarycafe

MORE GOOD CUPS

So many cool places to drink coffee ...

MAP № 74

THE SCANDINAVIAN COFFEE POD

The Studios, Royal Well Place, Cheltenham, Gloucestershire, GL50 3DN.

www.thescandinaviancoffeepod.com

MAP № 75

COTSWOLD ARTISAN COFFEE

5 Bishop's Walk, Cricklade Street, Cirencester, Gloucestershire, GL7 1JH.

MAP № 76

THE ROOKERY

35 Marlborough Street, Faringdon, Oxfordshire, SN7 7JL.

www.therookery.me.uk

MAP № 77

WATERLOO TEA - PENYLAN

5 Waterloo Gardens, Penylan, Cardiff, Wales, CF23 5AA.

www.waterlootea.com

MAP № 78

THE EARLY BIRD

38 Woodville Road, Cardiff, Wales, CF24 4EB.

www.earlybirdbakery.co.uk

MAP № 79

COFFI BANK

99 Wyverne Road, Cathays, Cardiff, Wales, CF24 4BG.

www.coffibank.co.uk

MAP № 80

BRODIES COFFEE CO

Gorsedd Gardens, Cathays Park, Cardiff, Wales, CF10 3NP.

www.brodiescoffee.co.uk

MAP № 81

KIN+ILK - CATHEDRAL ROAD

31 Cathedral Road, Pontcanna, Cardiff, Wales, CF11 9HB.

www.kinandilk.com

MAP № 82

ARTIGIANO - CARDIFF

16 Working Street, Cardiff, Wales, CF10 1GN.

www.artigiano.uk.com

MAP № 83

WATERLOO TEA - WYNDHAM

21-25 Wyndham Arcade, Cardiff, Wales, CF10 1FH.

www.waterlootea.com

No. 84
WATERLOO TEA - PENARTH
1-3 Washington Buildings,
Stanwell Road, Penarth,
Wales, CF64 2AD.

www.waterlootea.com

No. 85
CHANDOS DELI - BRISTOL
79 Henleaze Road, Bristol, BS9 4JP.

www.chandosdeli.com

No. 86
BAKERS AND CO
193 Gloucester Road, Bristol, BS7 8BG.

www.bakersbristol.co.uk

No. 87
CAFE RONAK
169 Gloucester Road, Bristol, BS7 8BE.

www.caferonak.co.uk

No. 88
BRISTOL COFFEE HOUSE
121 Whiteladies Road, Clifton,
Bristol, BS8 2PL.

www.bristolcoffeehouse.co.uk

No. 89
THE BRISTOLIAN CAFE
2 Picton Street, Montpelier,
Bristol, BS6 5QA.

www.thebristolian.co.uk

No. 90
SPICER+COLE - CLIFTON
9 Princess Victoria Street, Clifton
Village, Bristol, BS8 4BX.

www.spicerandcole.co.uk

No. 91
FRISKA - QUEEN'S ROAD
70 Queen's Road, Bristol, BS8 1QU.

www.friskafood.com

No. 92
BOSTON TEA PARTY - PARK STREET
75 Park Street, Bristol, BS1 5PF.

www.bostonteaparty.co.uk

No. 93
BEATROOT CAFE
20-21 Lower Park Row,
Bristol, BS1 5BN.

www.beatrootcafe.co.uk

MGC94
NO12 EASTON
12 High Street, Easton, Bristol, BS5 6DL.

www.12easton.com

MGC95
FULL COURT PRESS
59 Broad Street, Bristol, BS1 2EJ.

www.fcp.com

MGC96
CITY DELI
The Paragon, 32 Victoria Street, Bristol, BS1 6BX.

www.citydelibristol.co.uk

MGC98
SPICER+COLE - QUEEN SQUARE
1 Queen Square Avenue, Bristol, BS1 4JA.

www.spicerandcole.co.uk

MGC97
FRISKA - VICTORIA STREET
36 Victoria Street, Bristol, BS1 6BY.

www.friskafood.com

MGC99
THE GREEN BIRD CAFE
11 Margaret's Buildings, Bath, BA1 2LP.

www.greenbirdcafe.co.uk

MGC100
CHANDOS DELI - BATH
12 George Street, Bath, BA1 2EH.

www.chandosdeli.com

MGC101
HUNTER & SONS
Milsom Place, Bath, BA1 1BZ.

www.milsomplace.co.uk/food/hunter-sons

MGC102
GREEN ROCKET CAFE
1 Pierrepont Street, Bath, BA1 1LB.

www.thegreenrocket.co.uk

MGC103
THE FORUM COFFEE HOUSE
3-5 Forum Buildings,
St James's Parade, Bath, BA1 1UG.

www.bathforum.co.uk

MGC104
COFFEE LAB UK
35 Blue Boar Row, Salisbury,
Wiltshire, SP1 1DA.

www.coffeelabuk.com

MAP 105
SOUTH COAST ROAST
24 Richmond Hill, Bournemouth,
Dorset, BH2 6EJ.

www.thecaffeinehustler.com

MAP 106
THE DANCING GOAT
31 Parr Street, Poole,
Dorset, BH14 0JX.

www.thedancinggoat.co.uk

MAP 107
NUMBER 35 COFFEE HOUSE & KITCHEN
35 High West Street, Dorchester,
Dorset, DT1 1UP.

www.coffeehouseandkitchen.com

MAP 108
BOSTON TEA PARTY - HONITON
Monkton House, 53 High Street,
Honiton, Devon, EX14 1PW.

www.bostonteaparty.co.uk

MAP 109
ANNIE AND THE FLINT
126 High Street, Ilfracombe,
Devon, EX34 9EY.

www.annieandtheflint.co.uk

MAP 110
BOSTON TEA PARTY - BARNSTAPLE
21-22 Tuly Street, Barnstaple, Devon,
EX31 1DH.

www.bostonteaparty.co.uk

MAP 111
BIKE SHED CAFE
The Square, Barnstaple, Devon, EX32 8LS.

www.bikesheduk.com

MAP 112
CREDITON COFFEE COMPANY
1 Market Square House, Market
Street, Crediton, Devon, EX17 2BN.

www.creditoncoffee.co.uk

MAP 113
BOSTON TEA PARTY - EXETER
84 Queen Street, Exeter, Devon, EX4 3RP.

www.bostonteaparty.co.uk

MAP 114
DEVON COFFEE
88 Queen Street, Exeter, Devon,EX4 3RP.

www.devoncoffee.co.uk

MAP № 115
ARTIGIANO - EXETER
248 High Street, Exeter,
Devon, EX4 3PZ.

www.artigiano.uk.com

MAP № 116
CHANDOS DELI - EXETER
1 Roman Walk, Princesshay, Exeter,
Devon, EX1 1GN.

www.chandosdeli.com

MAP № 117
EXE COFFEE ROASTERS
19 Heavitree Road, Exeter,
Devon, EX1 2LD.

www.execoffeeroasters.co.uk

MAP № 118
CAFE AT 36
36 Cowick Street, Exeter,
Devon, EX4 1AW.

www.cafeat36.co.uk

MAP № 119
JACKA BAKERY
38 Southside Street, The Barbican,
Plymouth, Devon, PL1 2LE.

MAP № 120
OLIVE CO CAFE
Windsor Place, Liskeard, Cornwall, PL14 4BH.

www.olivecocafe.com

MAP № 121
RELISH FOOD & DRINK
Foundry Court, Wadebridge,
Cornwall, PL27 7QN.

www.relishcornwall.co.uk

MAP № 122
108 COFFEE HOUSE
108c Kenway Street, Truro,
Cornwall, TR1 3DJ.

www.108coffee.co.uk

MAP № 123
ESPRESSINI
39 Killigrew Street, Falmouth,
Cornwall, TR11 3PW.

www.espressini.co.uk

MAP № 124
ORIGIN COFFEE AT HARBOUR HEAD
Porthleven, Cornwall, TR13 9JY.

www.origincoffee.co.uk

EXPLODING BAKERY

№ 56

ROASTERS

ROASTWORKS COFFEE CO.
№ 139

ᴹᴬᴾ**125.** FOOTPRINT COFFEE

Ednol Farm, Kinnerton, Presteigne, Radnorshire, LD8 2PF.
www.footprintcoffee.co.uk   T: 01547 560177

f Footprint Coffee   y @footprintcoffee   @ @footprintcoffee

There's a pleasing synergy between Footprint's position halfway up a mountain in rural Wales and the coffee farms in the high altitudes of the tropical belt, from which its beans are sourced.

'We're probably the UK's highest coffee roastery,' says owner Emma Jones, *'which reflects the Footprint spirit of adventure'.*

Indeed Emma and husband/business partner Greg met while canoeing and spent two years travelling the length and breadth of the Americas. *'Greg had long held a passion for great coffee and, between mountain and wilderness adventures, we found ourselves seeking out the best indie coffee shops in North America,'* she says.

'IT WAS WHILE PARAGLIDING ABOVE THE COFFEE PLANTATIONS OF COLOMBIA THAT A PLAN WAS FORMED'

'We also had the opportunity to camp in Latin American coffee farms, living among the growers where we learned about coffee from the farmers' perspective – influencing our commitment to sourcing our beans ethically.'

However, it was while paragliding above the coffee plantations of Colombia, that a plan was born. *'So we dashed home, bought our first roaster and set about learning the art of speciality coffee roasting.'*

Sourcing single origin beans from across the world and roasting on Geoffrey, a state-of-the-art 15kg Giesen, the team is now producing award winning blends, including Call of the Wild and Muddy Boots, which recently won a Great Taste Award.

Wherever the beans are grown, Greg and Emma respect the growers' work and aim to roast each one in small batches to bring out the best of their individual qualities.

'Right now I'm excited about a beautiful washed Ethiopian called Biftu Gudina,' says Emma.

With the business serving trade and home brewers in equal measure, Footprint is turning up at cafes from Newcastle to Southampton as well as keeping consumers happy via its mail order and subscription services.

№126. JAMES GOURMET COFFEE CO

COFFEE COURSES AVAILABLE | COFFEE BEANS AVAILABLE ONLINE

Chase Industrial Estate, Alton Road, Ross-on-Wye, Herefordshire, HR9 5WA.

www.jamesgourmetcoffee.com   01989 566698

f James Gourmet Coffee Co Ltd   @gourmetpj   @jamesgourmetcoffee

'I got into roasting because I wasn't getting what I wanted out of the coffee I bought,' explains Peter James, the man behind one of the country's first independent, speciality coffee roasters.

'WE MAKE SURE THAT MORE IS SPENT ON GREEN BEANS THAN CORPORATE SWAGGER AND BRANDING'

'Back in the 1990s, I realised that coffee had the potential to be amazing, yet no one was really doing anything about it.'

Before 1999, Peter was originally a coffee packer, but grew tired of filling bags with below-par beans up to 21 hours a day. Roasting his own was the natural next step. 'People were roasting coffee until it tasted like charcoal, so we got our hands on a couple of roasters to see if we could do better.'

It certainly was better, and not just for the coffee lovers drinking James Gourmet at their local cafes. 'We've always aimed to buy the best coffee we can find and in doing so, connect people with the farmers whose beans we have sourced,' says Peter.

'We make sure a higher proportion of the money is spent on green beans rather than on corporate swagger and egotistical branding.'

With such an established coffee brand – you'll find James Gourmet's seasonal selection of blends and single origins in many of the best coffee shops and retailers across the country – the team continues to explore the boundaries of speciality beans.

'I think the next stage of coffee in this country is going to be fascinating,' beams Peter. 'It'll be more customer driven, with coffee drinkers leading the way with new favourites and seasonal varieties, rather than a few key influencers dictating what will be popular.'

ᵐᵃᵖ127. COALTOWN COFFEE ROASTERS

COFFEE COURSES AVAILABLE | COFFEE BEANS AVAILABLE | ONLINE | ONSITE

The Roastery, Glynhir Road, Ammanford, Carmarthenshire, Wales, SA18 2TB.
www.coaltowncoffee.co.uk   T: 01269 400105

f Coaltown Coffee Roasters   @coaltowncoffee   @coaltowncoffee

offee lovers of Wales and beyond are digging the scene at Coaltown Coffee Roasters in the former mining town of Ammanford.

Bringing "black gold" back to Carmarthenshire in the form of high grade arabica beans are roasters Gordon and Scott James – father and son (and great grandson to miner Ben Addis, whose image graces the Coaltown packaging).

Rooting the business firmly in their hometown in the Black Mountain, with its rich mining history, the chaps have earned their stripes, starting small on a homemade three kilo roaster (Gordon was previously an engineer), before moving on to a 12 kilo Probat. That's small stuff compared to the next step in their journey though, as they've just invested in a 75 kilo reconditioned UG75 Probat roaster from Italy, which from November will form the centrepiece at the new roastery, cafe and speciality coffee training school in Ammanford.

'We're creating an open roastery so that people can come and discover more about speciality coffee,' says Gordon, 'and drink our different espresso blends and single origins as espresso based coffees, pourovers and through syphon.'

'THE ROASTER WILL FORM THE CENTREPIECE OF THE NEW ROASTERY, CAFE AND SPECIALITY COFFEE TRAINING SCHOOL'

The two blends the roastery is currently best known for are its award winning, chocolatey, Black Gold No 3 blend and the more fruity Pit Prop No 1, which, says Gordon, 'is pushing the boundary a bit. We're roasting to meet the current Welsh palate, but educating all the time and introducing the market to new flavour profiles.'

128. LUFKIN COFFEE ROASTERS

COFFEE BEANS AVAILABLE / ONLINE / ONSITE

183a Kings Road, Cardiff, Wales, CF11 9DF.
www.lufkincoffee.com T: 07570 811764

f Lufkin Coffee Roasters   🐦 @lufkincoffee   📷 @lufkincoffee

After a string of coffee gigs in California and developing a taste for speciality in his hometown of San Francisco, the Welsh capital isn't the first place that you'd expect seasoned barista Dan Lukins to set up his first solo project.

But when his wife Frances got an offer to study ceramics in the city, the duo discovered a lack of great filter and decided to set up Cardiff's first speciality roastery dedicated to the brew bar.

'I WAS ROASTING BACK-TO-BACK INTO THE SMALL HOURS, ONE KILOGRAM AT A TIME'

Launching in September 2015, Lufkin was an instant hit with the thriving local indie scene. 'I'd got a good deal on a 1kg roaster from some guys in London and thought it would be the ideal first set-up,' explains Dan, 'but it just went mad. I couldn't keep up with demand and was roasting back-to-back into the small hours, one kilogram at a time.'

Luckily for Cardiff's coffee fiends, the piccolo roaster was upgraded to a lungo model, with a 10kg Datgen DR10 now keeping the neighbourhood cafes and farmers' markets stocked with its rotating single origin offering. 'While a blend isn't off the table, we're pretty passionate about single origin. There's so much to learn and discover about each single estate's crop and their own inherent flavour notes,' adds Frances.

Currently, the best place to sip the speciality beans is at the Pontcanna roastery and stylish brew bar, which serves a small selection of edible treats alongside Dan's cracking coffee.

Stick around and watch the guys working on the next batch, grab a coffee to-go or make a visit when the courtyard comes alive during the monthly farmers' market, where you can stock up on beans, pick up a couple of bottles of craft beer from the micro brewery next door and lovely local veg from the stalls.

129. RAVE COFFEE

Unit 7, Stirling Works, Love Lane, Cirencester, Gloucestershire, GL7 1YG.

www.ravecoffee.co.uk   T: 01285 651884

f RAVE Coffee   🐦 @ravecoffee   ✉ @ravecoffee

RAVE's story begins like a few other roasters and cafes in this guide, with two ex-pats in Oz – Vikki and Rob Hodge in this particular tale – some barista classes and roasting tutorials, countless hours in Sydney's speciality coffee shops and a dream of taking this coffee culture home to the UK.

Impressively, they did it, and for five years have been keeping a notable catalogue of speciality shops, top restaurants and hotel chains expertly caffeinated with their responsibly sourced, delicious coffee.

'THE GUYS HAVE ALSO GOT AN OUTPOST IN CANADA'

Specialising in new crop seasonal coffees, roasting is approached with a constant rotation to show off each bean's best attributes. *'This year we're mixing things up a little,'* explains head roaster Brooke Purdon.

'Instead of ordering large lots of green beans (once we've whittled down the best samples), we're buying in smaller quantities to ensure the coffee is as fresh as possible. Now each bag of greens is usually out of the door within three months.'

This quick turnaround also means a speedier rotation of seasonal single origins for RAVE's coffee subscribers and stockists to get stuck into. *'We've been roasting like mad this past year,'* Brooke continues, *'and we've found loads of fantastic new coffees such as the Colombian Finca Tamana and the Ethiopian Layo Tiraga, which is stunning.'*

With a cafe at the Cotswolds HQ, enthusiasts can indulge in the sights, sounds and smells of a working roastery while sampling the team's latest showstopper. Plus, the guys have also got an outpost in Alberta, Canada if you're ever in that neck of the woods.

THE ART AND SCIENCE
OF ROASTING

№130. EXTRACT COFFEE ROASTERS

COFFEE COURSES AVAILABLE | COFFEE BEANS AVAILABLE | ONLINE ONSITE

Unit 1, Gatton Road, Bristol, BS2 9SH.

www.extractcoffee.co.uk   T: 01179 554976

f Extract Coffee Roasters   🐦 @extractcoffee   📷 @extractcoffee

Continuing its work to close the gap between farmer and coffee drinker, a trip to the Santa Barbara Estates in Colombia made for an exciting start to 2016 for Bristol-based Extract Coffee Roasters.

The passionate team behind the family-run roastery hasn't always been plane hopping between farms in exotic destinations. Like the majority of indie roasters, Extract started out selling its home roasted coffee from a small cart in the city centre.

Fast forward seven years and the team of coffee enthusiasts now work from an artisan roastery, which has been restored and built by hand and is equipped with refurbished roasters including Betty, its 1955 vintage Probat roaster.

Extract's love of learning has been the driving force behind its recent trips to origin. These excursions have resulted in a number of delicious new collaborations and innovative projects, such as insightful talks and seminars with the farmers for the entire Extract team and their industry friends. Speakers so far have included Boyce Harries from the Chania Estate in Kenya and Pedro Echavarria from the Santa Barbara Estates in Colombia.

'THE CREW HAS BEEN MUCKING IN AT GLASTONBURY AND SPREADING THE SPECIALITY WORD'

Extract's team of trainers continue to progress too, with head of coffee training and development, Dan Lacey, acquiring the SCAE Coffee Diploma earlier this year, kick starting the new SCAE training programme at the roastery.

The crew have also been mucking in at festivals across the South West including Glastonbury, where they've been serving top-quality coffee and spreading the speciality word. With more events in the pipeline, new coffees to be launched and more work with the farmers at origin in the planner, there's plenty more to look forward to from Extract over the next year.

131. CLIFTON COFFEE ROASTERS

Unit C2, Island Trade Park, Bristow Broadway, Avonmouth, Bristol, BS11 9FB.
www.cliftoncoffee.co.uk   T: 01179 820252

f Clifton Coffee Roasters   🐦 @cliftoncoffee   📷 @cliftoncoffee

Since its launch in 2001, Clifton Coffee Roasters has built an enviable reputation as one of the region's leading independent roasters of speciality coffee, as well as machinery suppliers and coffee educators.

From its base just outside of Bristol, the team has over 100 years combined experience in the industry.

Head of coffee, Andy Tucker, manages the supply chain which includes Clifton's own direct relationships with producers in El Salvador as well as working with speciality importers to source unique and distinctive coffees on a seasonal basis.

From its state-of-the-art training facility, leading UK barista Jimmy Dimitrov also delivers an education programme that includes a variety of courses as part of the SCAE Diploma.

'The aim is to ensure that our customers are supported to serve the best possible cup of coffee,' says Andy.

'As well as a tailored education programme developed to specific customer needs, we offer an extensive in-house engineering service that covers the UK across the entire range of equipment we sell.' That includes leading manufacturers such as La Marzocco, Victoria Arduino, La Spaziale, Compak, Fetco and Mahlkonig.

Clifton's coffees can be found in some of the finest cafes, bars, restaurants and hotels across the country – from Cornwall to London and into Scotland. From its spiritual home in Bristol, Clifton remains at the forefront of the South West coffee industry and is a proud founding sponsor of the *South West Independent Coffee Guide*.

'FROM ITS BASE JUST OUTSIDE OF BRISTOL, THE TEAM HAS OVER 100 YEARS COMBINED EXPERIENCE IN THE INDUSTRY'

 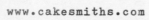 www.cakesmiths.com

EST 2014
BAKED IN BRISTOL

cakesmithsHQ #Cakesmiths.HQ @CakesmithsHQ

№132. ROUND HILL ROASTERY

Unit 14, Midsomer Enterprise Park, Midsomer Norton, Somerset, BA3 2BB.

www.roundhillroastery.com T: 01761 418808

f Round Hill Roastery 🐦 @roundhillcoffee 📷 @roundhillroastery

Things are taking off big time for talented Somerset based roaster Eddie Twitchett. His star has been in the ascendent since he started Round Hill in 2012, and the roastery now supplies many leading lights on the coffee scene, in the South West and way beyond too.

Developments this year include a new roastery with a swanky training area with Sanremo Opera machines and EK grinders, to provide quality control as well as giving customers somewhere to learn.

'IN ADDITION, EDDIE'S BEEN ON SOME INTREPID TRIPS TO SOURCE COFFEE AT ORIGIN, MOST NOTABLY IN COLOMBIA'

There's also new packaging for the beans to reflect the roasting style: pink for brightness, acidity and sweetness in the espressos and blue to indicate clean, pure and elegant filters.

In addition, Eddie's been on some intrepid trips to source coffee at origin, most notably to Colombia which has resulted in a focus on buying greens from that region.

'We visited farms that we've bought from over the past few years and also took the opportunity to source some new ones too,' he says.

'We were impressed with the processing experiments carried out at Santa Barbara Estate by the Echavarria family. They own five farms and this year we focused on Veracruz and San Pascual. We also made sure to visit Finca la Julia – a coffee we have bought for four years now.'

It's not all about Colombia though, as the guys also hope to get to Brazil, Kenya and Ethiopia next year, while buying from other coffee producing countries too.

'Wherever we source from, we're careful to complement the hard work already put in by the farmers,' says Eddie. *'We focus on each coffee's unique character and roast to highlight its natural flavours and sweetness.'*

№ 133. DUSTY APE

Marsh Farm Roastery, Hilperton, Wiltshire, BA14 7PJ.

www.dustyape.com T: 01225 753838

f Dusty Ape 🐦 @dustyape 📷 @dustyape

With big plans to move to a new, more spacious unit and bring an old vintage roaster back to life this year, there are exciting times ahead for Wiltshire's Dusty Ape.

The Ape was born with a tiny roaster in the garden shed even before founder Phil Buckley quit his corporate career. *'Almost by chance, I got a taste of the coffee industry when I landed a software project with Costa. Although the project was deeply rewarding, I knew I much preferred the coffee I roasted myself,'* explains Phil.

Four years on and the award winning roastery now hand-crafts up to 10 single origins and single estates alongside its three blends – Molten Toffee, Silverback Espresso and Capuchin – on its 12kg Probat Probatone and 5kg Toper roasters.

'Sourcing coffees seasonally, the key is knowing what we are after for a particular brew method, meticulously cupping many samples until we find it and then buying the best, hopefully before it's all sold,' says Phil. *'Good coffees don't hang around for long.'*

'We've recently started inviting our customers and local coffee enthusiasts to our cupping sessions,' continues Phil. *'It's great to get their input on flavour notes as they're the ones who are going to be enjoying the yield.'*

'WE'VE RECENTLY STARTED INVITING OUR CUSTOMERS AND LOCAL COFFEE ENTHUSIASTS TO OUR CUPPING SESSIONS'

'There have been some fantastic finds this year including Wenago, a natural Ethiopian Yirgacheffe and Karatina, a Kenyan peaberry with delicious dark fruit notes. We've also just rediscovered an old favourite from the Las Delicias Estate located in the golden coffee belt of El Salvador.'

Stocking an increasing number of speciality cafes across the South West and beyond, as well as keeping home enthusiasts expertly caffeinated with their subscription service, Phil and team make sure every cup reaches the full flavour potential, with hands-on advice and training for all their customers.

№134. SQUARE ROOT COFFEE

COFFEE BEANS AVAILABLE ONSITE

12 Station Yard, Edington, Wiltshire, BA13 4NT.
www.squarerootcoffee.com   T 07940 120835

f Square Root Coffee   🐦 @sqrootcoffee

After gaining 20 years of experience in the brewing industry, Adrian Smith turned his craft from hops to green beans in 2012 when the opportunity arose to take his enthusiasm for speciality coffee to the next level.

'Exploring the alchemy of the green bean and experimenting with roasting processes at home, my family and friends became my test subjects when I was starting out,' explains Adrian. *'Their feedback on new beans, blends and roast profiles gave me the confidence to turn a passion into a livelihood.'*

Highlighting similarities between the craft beer and speciality coffee movement, Adrian drew on his experience to detect complex flavours and aromas derived from different beans, and after an extensive amount of cupping, created Square Root's first signature blend, The Solution.

'Speciality coffee is a food product and should be treated with the same respect afforded to the very finest food. We explore all of the taste nuances of each batch to find the sweet spot and sample roasts until we find the perfect combination.'

Sourcing solely arabica beans from respected green bean importers around the world, Adrian also roasts a number of seasonal coffees on the 3kg drum roaster – affectionately known as Laura – from the micro roastery in the charming village of Edington.

'SQUARE ROOT'S LATEST YIELD CAN BE SAMPLED AT ITS SPECIALITY SHOP IN BATH'

Square Root's latest yield can be sampled at its first speciality shop on Bath's Kingsmead Square, where you'll often find Adrian armed with the latest tasting notes and coffee recommendations. Don't despair if you can't make it to the historic city as all of Adrian's small batch roasted beans are also available online as one-off indulgences or monthly subscriptions.

135. SOUTH COAST ROAST COFFEE ROASTERS

24 Richmond Hill, Bournemouth, Dorset, BH2 6EJ.
www.thecaffienehustler.com | 01202 551197

f South Coast Roast The Roastery 🐦 @southcoastroast 📷 @scr_coffee_roasters

It's only to be expected that the same passion driving two of Bournemouth's pioneer coffee shops would spill over into roasting, training and consultancy work.

Boscanova and sister cafe South Coast Roast are popular hotspots in the town for decent brekkies, brunches and brews. Yet these hipster joints not only deliver all that's worth seeking out in indie coffee shops but now have a growing reputation for their roastery too.

South Coast Coffee Roasters, which is due to move into new premises in the town's Triangle, is where head roaster Heather Anderson showcases single origin green beans and blended concoctions.

'We like to serve a range of coffee at our cafes with a consistent espresso blend and a changing guest espresso,' she says.

Heather also likes to mix it up with either a blend or single origin for the filter coffee.

'I feel like we can be a bit more adventurous with the flavours in filters (especially via the Clever dripper) and get people to try something fruity or floral that they may not expect,' she says.

The roastery offers barista, latte art and cupping courses, along with Latte Art Sprodowns where coffee enthusiasts and local cafes are invited to compete in a 'very casual' latte art competition. 'It's been an amazing way to meet a few of the local coffee gang.'

'THE ROASTERY OFFERS BARISTA, LATTE ART AND CUPPING COURSES, ALONG WITH LATTE ART SPRODOWNS'

Heather has worked as a barista in both cafes for a decade and says: 'it's been an incredible experience moving from barista to roaster and a huge learning curve, although the short chain between the roastery and the cafes means we get instant feedback.'

MAP N°136. READS COFFEE

Limekiln Farm, Thornford Road, Sherborne, Dorset, DT9 6PS.

www.readscoffee.co.uk T: 01935 481010

f Reads Coffee Roasters 🐦 @reads_coffee 📷 @readscoffeeroasters

A s the guy behind Pret's original foray into coffee, (following a few years catching the coffee bug in Vancouver 26 years ago), Giles Dick-Read certainly has the experience to help coffee businesses at a strategic level. However, it was after working with large roasteries that he decided to make the move into small scale speciality roasting with his wife Charlotte.

Now, from supplying a wide range of coffees to providing the training and equipment with which to serve it, the Dick-Read family business has evolved into more than just a cottage industry. *'We started roasting 14 years ago, maybe one of importer Mercanta's earlier customers'* says Giles. *'We've grown steadily, developing all the time through word of mouth'.*

Now Reads offers a range of single origin coffees from around the world and up to 14 coffees in total. *'We tend to roast coffee the way we like to drink it,'* says Giles.

'We're not necessarily ones for following particular trends so, for example, our Firehouse Espresso uses an element of washed robusta to give it the power that many of our customers are looking for'.

'WE TEND TO ROAST COFFEE THE WAY WE LIKE TO DRINK IT'

Indeed roasting espresso is a big part of the business with a significant amount heading to London.

Not that there's anything remotely urban about the Reads HQ, which is situated on a working farm on the edge of Sherborne in rural Dorset. In a converted dairy next to the cow shed, you'll find Giles at the 25kg Probat and 12kg Ambex roasters, Sue and Sam bagging and labelling, and Emma and Charlotte looking after the customers and marketing from an office that not so long ago housed the milk tank. It's more haybarn than hipster, and thoroughly charming for it.

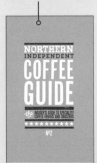

MAP № 137. BRAZIER COFFEE ROASTERS

COFFEE COURSES AVAILABLE | COFFEE BEANS AVAILABLE | ONLINE | ONSITE

The Puttee House, Tonedale Business Park, Tonedale, Wellington, Somerset, TA21 0AW.

www.braziercoffeeroasters.co.uk　T: 01823 352217

f Brazier Coffee Roasters　🐦 @brazierroasters　📷 @braziercoffeeroasters

High altitude coffee specialists Brazier may be roasting from the flat terrain of the Somerset levels, but things are certainly on the rise.

When last year's guide came out, Tom and Claire Brazier's business was only seven months old and had five serious customers. Now it's got 40, with four people working in the business.

'THERE ARE BIG PLANS AFOOT FOR A MODERNIST BRAZIER CAFE IN SOMERSET'

New developments include an origin trip to Indonesia last year, the introduction of machine supply and servicing, becoming Fairtrade certified, and a tantalising opportunity to exclusively import cool coffee gear from Claire's native Oz.

'We're doing things properly with an eye on quality all the time,' says Tom. In coffee terms, that translates as the team focusing on buying green beans from small importers who specialise in just one country of origin. *'There's lots to tell customers about coffee, but you can't teach everything at once, so the first message we're aiming to get across is about geography and the specific farms the coffee comes from.'*

The Brazier blends include the flagship speciality Altitude blend and the Seasonal blend, which, says Tom, *'is fairly light but with a more general profile. We use whatever is in season, which gives us the opportunity to talk about seasonality'.* There's also a Fairtrade blend which is a slightly darker roast. The coffee is only currently available for trade, but there are big plans afoot for a move to a larger combined roastery and cafe at the historic Tonedale Mill development near Wellington. Visitors will be able to drop in for a takeaway coffee or linger longer over a brew while observing the fascinating roasting process taking place. Watch this space.

ᴹᴬᴾᴺᵒ **138.** COFFEE FACTORY

Unit 3, Samurai Buildings, Seaton Junction, Axminster, Devon, EX13 7PW.
www.coffeefactory.co.uk ⏐ 01297 551259

f Coffee Factory 🐦 @coffee_factory ⬚ @coffee_factory

Coffee Factory started out as a family business with just one aim – to offer incredible coffees and make them accessible. And it's a formula that is obviously working.

Flagship blend Black Bear has won both Great Taste and Taste of the West awards while its exclusive single estate Bosque Lye (orange bourbon) from El Salvador is proving a massive hit with its customers.

'CUPPING AND CHOOSING OUR SINGLE ORIGIN COFFEES IS THE MOST EXCITING PART OF THE WEEK'

The artisan roastery's mission to create a masterpiece in every mug involves sourcing some of the best tasting seasonal beans the world has to offer before crafting them into coffees that provide a consistent taste profile all year round.

For head roaster Danny Parfitt that doesn't mean just setting the timer and walking away from the roaster. This is a minute-by-minute process where every change in texture, appearance, aroma and sound is monitored in a beautifully restored 1950s Probat machine, affectionately known as Dorothy.

'Cupping and choosing our single origin coffees is the most exciting part of our week,' says Danny, who has worked as a chef and barista. *'We simply pick our favourites so all our customers can enjoy them too.'*

A factory cafe within the roastery is not just a place to get decent coffee and cake but also to watch the beans releasing their diversity of exciting flavours and aromas.

The main emphasis for this year is the Coffee Factory subscription service for the home coffee addict, which has been growing since 2011, with the Roasters Choice and Discovery Pack being big hits. The roastery aims to launch its new website this year combining the best of Coffee Factory and Bean and Ground services and products.

☰ 139. ROASTWORKS COFFEE CO.

Unit 7, Blackdown Park, Willand, Devon, EX15 2FS.

www.roastworks.co.uk T: **01884 829400**

f Roastworks Coffee Co. 🐦 @roastworksdevon 📷 @roastworks_coffee_co

THE LAB

Y ou've got to love the chutzpah of Will Little of Roastworks. Seeing what roasters Origin had done in Cornwall, and Clifton and Extract had created in Bristol, he identified a gap in the market for a Devon-based roaster with intentions as a serious player.

Step one was to renovate the *'badass'* vintage German G W Barth drum roaster that had been in the family for 30 years. Step two was to move into a 3,000 sq ft warehouse outside Exeter, close to the family business [Little's Coffee]. Then, step three (with wife and business partner Caroline) was to turn the echoing space into something rather cool with a test cafe and training area, plus room for public cuppings and other events.

Utilising beautiful design (Will was formerly a graphic designer and Caroline a fashion designer) the pair have created something significant out of what was just an opportunity.

'WILL IDENTIFIED A GAP IN THE MARKET FOR A DEVON-BASED ROASTER WITH INTENTIONS AS A SERIOUS PLAYER'

And when you add Roastworks foray into the hugely developing world of coffee capsules (of the speciality variety, naturally), as yet another way of, *'engaging more consumers in third wave, speciality coffee,'* this is most definitely one to watch.

№140. CRANKHOUSE COFFEE

Great Matridge, Longdown, Exeter, Devon, EX6 7BE.
www.crankhousecoffee.co.uk T: 07588 020288

f Crankhouse Coffee 🐦 @crankhouseroast 📷 @crankhouseroast

The Crankhouse wheels have been accelerating this year with a move to new roasting premises, providing more space for training and cupping classes, as well as a retail area for beans which are sporting colourful new packaging.

Dave's recently taken his first origin trip to El Salvador as the harvest was concluding, with ripe cherries still on the trees. And it was there that he established a relationship with three growers that he looks to develop further in the future. This year he purchased two coffees from Finca las Nubes in Santa Ana.

'WHEN YOU ARE ON THE SLOPES AMONG THE CHERRIES, PUTTING THEM IN YOUR MOUTH AND TASTING THEM ... THAT'S INCREDIBLE'

'Being in El Salvador joined the dots for me,' he says. *'I felt like I was at the heart of coffee.'*

'It's all well and good reading books and watching YouTube but when you are on the slopes among the cherries, putting them in your mouth and tasting them ... that's incredible. I think anyone who works in speciality coffee should go – it's a necessary part of the education process.'

Crankhouse has a frequently changing list of seasonal single origins and blends, some of which pay homage to Dave's road-cycling interest, such as the Grand Tour Blend and the Spring Classic Blend. *'I use a variety of importers and select the coffees after extensive sample roasting and cupping,'* he says, *'as my aim is to offer a variety of origin, processing and flavour profiles for my customers to enjoy.'*

141. VOYAGER COFFEE ROASTERS

Unit 6, Mardle Way Business Park, Buckfastleigh, Devon, TQ11 0JL.

www.voyager.coffee   T: 01364 644440

f Voyager Coffee Roasters   🐦 @voyagercoffee   📷 @voyagercoffee

Voyager's Round the World Tasting Club is bringing exciting new flavours to its customers. Carefully selected beans from across the globe – with tasting notes – are showcased monthly and delivered straight to regulars' doors.

'I find it exciting because I can get in a really nice coffee and experiment with it,' says head roaster Rachael Jowitt. *'It's a gesture to our regular customers so they get a little sample of something they wouldn't otherwise try, alongside their usual blend'*

Since joining the business last year, Rachael has seen more and more cafes, hotels and restaurants across the South West seek out Voyager's outstanding espresso blends, including Kaldi's Oddyssey, which holds a Taste of the West gold award.

'We now hand-roast our coffee using a state-of-the-art 30kg Genio roaster – the first ever to be made by the South African company – which makes production more efficient and enjoyable.'

Rachael makes a point of listening to customers in her pursuit of great tasting coffee, saying: *'it's about helping our*

customers invigorate peoples' daily lives with coffee and educating them to get the best out of it.'

Being a good roaster, she believes, requires great attention to detail and a developed sense of taste.

'IT'S ABOUT HELPING OUR CUSTOMERS INVIGORATE PEOPLES' DAILY LIVES WITH COFFEE'

'We have been on sensory courses and it's quite amazing how you can develop your palate through regular educational cupping sessions,' says Rachael, who holds weekly tasting sessions with the team.

Founded by managing director Andrew Tucker, the roastery offers customers a full bean-to-cup experience. At its headquarters in Buckfastleigh, accredited barista training courses are run in the swish state-of-the-art academy. Voyager is also a Sanremo espresso machine distributor, helping businesses across the South West benefit from a full range of leading equipment.

№142. SABINS SMALL BATCH ROASTERS

Butterfly Barn, Hersham, Bude, Cornwall, EX23 9LZ.
www.sabinscoffee.co.uk   T: 01288 321660

f Sabins Coffee   f @sabinscoffee   @ @sabins_coffee

Emma and Paul Sabin have a quirky claim to fame: they were the first Brits to put an espresso machine on a trike.

In the early days, the two could be spotted pedalling around the Kent countryside, selling coffees to flagging tourists walking the coastal path. This delightful mobile-catering contraption, called The Tradecycle, was subsequently featured in episodes of *The Apprentice* and *EastEnders*.

Today, the Cornish roasters still like to bring innovative creativity to the coffee business. Their roastery is an adorable shed, tucked away on their smallholding in a secluded Cornish hamlet.

'THE WHOLE FAMILY WILL ARGUE QUITE CREATIVELY BEFORE WE HIT THE SWEET SPOT'

From this back garden beauty, Paul works his alchemy on green beans, turning them into bags of coffee goodness to supply local cafes, restaurants, retailers and their online shop.

Yet it's not just Paul who has a say in the final product, as it's very much a family business. Eldest daughter Florence is a barista while Lily, Rose, Fyn, Noah and Jonah are all trainees in the taste trade.

'*Daddy will roast and Florence and I will be cupping,*' says Emma. '*The whole family will argue quite creatively before we hit the sweet spot.*'

The couple source arabica beans from cooperatives, micro lots and single origins, using certified organic, Fairtrade or Rainforest Alliance beans as much as possible. It's a journey of endless flavours from across the globe as they have just received their first sample of directly sourced wild coffee from an archipelago in the Indian Ocean.

They are also resolutely proud to be small roasters. '*We are going to stay as small batch roasters even if we need to get two roasters,*' says Paul. '*If we start upping the game, it would change what we want to achieve.*'

143. OLFACTORY COFFEE ROASTERS

COFFEE COURSES AVAILABLE | COFFEE BEANS AVAILABLE | ONLINE | ONSITE

The Old Brewery Yard, Lower Treluswell, Penryn, Cornwall, TR10 9AT.

www.olfactorycoffee.co.uk   T 01326 259980

f Olfactory Coffee Roasters   🐦 @olfactorycoffee   ⊙ @olfactorycoffee

A welcoming and informal open-door policy at Olfactory Coffee Roasters makes it a fascinating stop-off for anyone curious to learn more about the craft of roasting speciality coffee.

'We take what we do really seriously but, apart from that, nothing else is serious here,' says Benjamin Jenkin who, as part of a busy team of five, is head of training as well as roasting and bean sourcing. *'We are super informal and anyone can pop in. I have been in coffee for a few years now and you can get intimidated by the industry, but that's just not what we are about.'*

'ETHICS ARE ALWAYS HIGH ON THE AGENDA WHEN IT COMES TO WORKING WITH FARMERS AND GREEN BEAN BROKERS'

Set up in 2013 by owner Angel Parushev, the roastery, housed in a former brewery on the outskirts of Penryn, is devoted to finding the best seasonal speciality coffees the world has to offer, while bringing out the characteristics, flavour and sweetness of each bean.

A newly-built training room is where coffee enthusiasts come to discover more about freshly-roasted beans from Kenya, Rwanda, Tanzania, Colombia and El Salvador as well as to taste them at the machines.

'When we are training we like to give people the chance to try the coffee so they can find out what they like,' says Benjamin.

Small-batch seasonal espressos like Knock Out and Jackrock contribute to Cornwall's speciality coffee culture while bestselling filter coffees, such as Finca Los Nogales, are popular with the home market.

Ethics are always high on the agenda, especially when it comes to working with farmers and green-bean brokers. *'We adhere to pretty strict environmental and social protocols,'* adds Benjamin, who has an MSc in environmental science. *'It's all about working closely with our importers and using them as a gateway to learning all we can about the consequences of sourcing.'*

MAP № 144. ORIGIN COFFEE

COFFEE COURSES AVAILABLE | COFFEE BEANS AVAILABLE | ONLINE | ONSITE

The Roastery, Wheal Vrose Business Park, Helston, Cornwall, TR13 0FG.
www.origincoffee.co.uk   T: 01326 574337

f Origin Coffee Roasters   🐦 @origincoffee   @ @origincoffeeroasters

To say it's been a busy year for the guys at Origin Coffee would be something of an understatement.

Not only has the Helston-based roastery continued to increase production of its speciality coffees and popped up in even more of our favourite coffee shops across the country, but the tight team of coffee professionals has also opened two new coffee shops in London, relaunched its website (which includes helpful home brew films), introduced a bottled cold brew, and taken some seriously exciting sourcing trips - Honduras and Colombia to name just two. And, to top it off, their head of wholesale, Dan Fellows, became the 2016 UK Barista Champion.

However, all of this success and expansion hasn't stopped owner Tom Sobey and team from keeping up Origin's impeccably high standards and ethical integrity.

'We direct trade around 90% of our coffee,' explains Tom, 'working closely with long term producer partners whom we visit regularly. We also have collaborative importer partnerships, enabling us to showcase coffees from incredible producing countries such as Kenya and Ethiopia.'

Roasting on two Loring Smart Roasts, Origin currently stocks speciality shops from Cornwall to Scotland with two espresso blends, two mainstay single origins, a decaf and a monthly featured coffee.

Launching new sensory skills modules in its coffee education programme this year, Origin's SCAE certified trainers are two of only six to teach these in the UK.

'The incredible dedication of the team is pretty impressive,' adds Tom. 'We're proud to have some of the most awarded people in the industry.'

'TO TOP IT OFF, THEIR HEAD OF WHOLESALE, DAN FELLOWS, BECAME THE 2016 UK BARISTA CHAMPION'

MAP Nᵒ 145. ANTLER AND BIRD

COFFEE BEANS AVAILABLE ONSITE

Bramleys, Bournes Green, Stroud, Gloucestershire, GL6 7NL.
www.antlerandbird.co.uk   T: 07921 924809

f Antler & Bird Cold Brew   🐦 @antlerandbird   📷 @antlerandbird

Born out of an ambition to create an accessible and high quality chilled coffee – you know, one not tainted by UHT milk and sweetened to the high heavens – Antler and Bird is the cold brew creation of two coffee lovers from the Cotswolds.

After working in Bath as a barista, co-owner Theo Garcia went on to win the Welsh AeroPress Championship in 2016, before teaming up with fellow coffee enthusiast, and pop-up business pro, Alex Foss-Sims. The duo spent six months brewing before they were finally happy to launch their *'no milk, no sugar, no nonsense brew'*.

'WE'RE SUCKERS FOR THE SL-28: STRAWBERRIES, BLACKCURRANTS AND CITRUS'

To maintain the quality, the guys buy beans in small quantities and hold regular cupping sessions to identify which seasonal varietals will come up trumps at the end of the cold brew process.

'Kenyans tend to win most of the time as we're suckers for the SL-28: strawberries, blackcurrants and citrus,' says Theo.

After steeping the ground coffee in filtered water for 16-20 hours, the result is a seriously refreshing and naturally sweet brew to be enjoyed at the crack of a bottle top. The beautifully designed bottles are currently available at a number of shops, cafes and delis across the South West and in three London branches of Daylesford Organic.

MORE GOOD ROASTERS

MAP № 149

EXE COFFEE ROASTERS

19 Heavitree Road, Exeter, Devon, EX1 2LD.

www.execoffeeroasters.co.uk

MAP № 146

LITTLE AND LONG COFFEE ROASTERS

Unit 50, Station Road Workshops, Station Road, Bristol, BS15 4PJ.

www.littleandlong.com

MAP № 150

LITTLESTONE COFFEE

17 Norman Court, Budlake Road, Exeter, Devon, EX2 8PY.

www.littlestonecoffee.co.uk

MAP № 148

ROASTED RITUALS COFFEE

Unit 18, Kenn Court Business Park, Roman Farm Road, Bristol, BS4 1UL.

www.roastedritualscoffee.com

MAP № 147

TWO DAY COFFEE ROASTERS

135 St Michael's Hill, Bristol, BS2 8BS.

www.twodaycoffee.co.uk

MAP № 151

YALLAH COFFEE

Argal Home Farm, Kergilliack, Falmouth, Cornwall, TR11 5PD.

www.yallahcoffee.co.uk

THE MANY STAGES OF
THE COFFEE BEAN

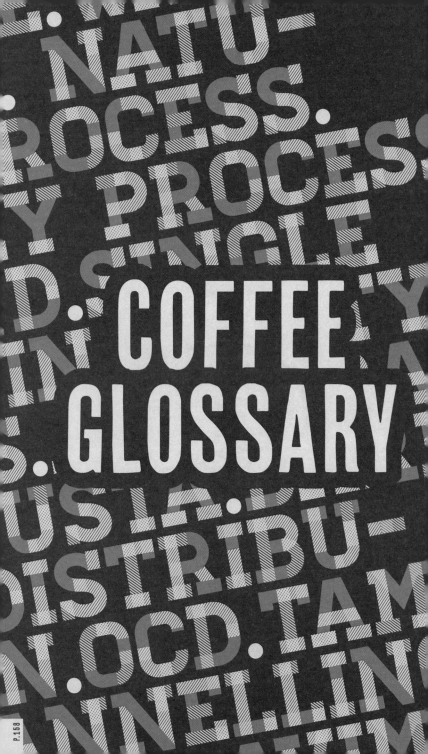

COFFEE GLOSSARY

ESPRESSO

BARISTA

The multi-skilled pro making your delicious coffee drinks.

CHANNELING

When a small hole or crack in the coffee bed of espresso forms, resulting in the water bypassing the majority of the ground coffee.

DISTRIBUTION

The action of distributing coffee evenly inside the espresso basket before tamping to encourage even extraction. This can be achieved through tapping, shaking or smoothing the coffee out with your fingers.

DOSE

The amount of ground coffee used when preparing a coffee.

GOD-SHOT

The name given to a shot of espresso when all the variables are in line and the coffee tastes at its optimum.

GRAVIMETRIC

The term for an espresso machine with the technology to control the yield, based on coffee dose.

OCD

Tool used for distributing coffee inside the espresso.

PRESSURE PROFILING

The act of controlling the amount of pressure applied to espresso throughout the extraction time, resulting in different espresso flavours and styles.

ROSETTA

The name given to the fern-like latte art pattern served on the top of a flat white or other milk drink.

TAMP

The action of compacting coffee into the espresso basket with a tamper in order to encourage even extraction.

YIELD

The volume of liquid produced when preparing an espresso or brewed coffee. A traditional espresso would yield twice that of the coffee dose. For example if you use 18g of coffee to brew an espresso, then you might yield 36g of liquid.

FILTER

AGITATE
Stirring the coffee throughout the brew cycle when preparing filter coffee to increase strength or encourage even extraction.

BATCH BREW
Filter coffee prepared on a large scale using a filter coffee machine.

BLOOM
The action of pouring water on freshly ground coffee to evenly coat each coffee particle. This encourages even extraction.

BREW
The general term given to filter coffee – as opposed to espresso.

CASCARA
The outer skin of the coffee cherry can be used to make an infusion served hot like a tea or cold, mixed with sparkling water.

COFFEE BLOSSOM
The flowers collected from the coffee bush are dried and can be used to make a tea-like infusion.

COLD BREW
Coffee brewed using cold water and left to extract over a longer period. Served cold, this coffee has high sweetness and low acidity.

CUPPING
The international method used to assess coffee. The beans are ground to a coarse consistency and steeped in a bowl of hot water for four minutes before the crust of grounds is scraped away from the surface. The coffee is left to cool and assessed via a big slurp from a cupping spoon.

EK43
Popular grinder used for both espresso and filter.

BEANS

ARABICA

The species of coffee commonly associated with speciality coffee, arabica is a delicate species which grows at high altitudes. It has lower levels of caffeine and typically higher perceived acidity, sweetness and a cleaner body.

BLEND

A blend of coffee from different farms and origins, traditionally used for espresso.

HONEY PROCESS

This process sits in-between washed and natural. The seeds are removed from the cherry and then left to dry with the mucilage intact, resulting in a sweet coffee with some characteristics of washed and natural process coffee.

NATURAL PROCESS

Naturally processed coffee is picked from the coffee bush and left to rest for a period of time with the fruit of the coffee cherry intact. In some cases the cherry can be left like this for two weeks before being hulled off. This results in a fruity, full body.

NINETY PLUS

All coffee is graded before sale with points out of 100. Speciality coffee will have 80 or more points. A coffee with 90 or more points is referred to as 90+ and will usually be quite exclusive, very tasty and expensive!

ROBUSTA

A low grade species of coffee, robusta grows at lower altitudes. This species has a high caffeine content and displays more bitterness and earthy flavours.

SINGLE ORIGIN

The term usually used for coffee from one origin. Single estate is the term used for coffee from one farm. Can be used for espresso or filter.

WASHED

Washed coffee is picked from the coffee bush and the outer layers of the cherry are immediately removed from the seed (what you normally call the coffee bean) and put into fermentation tanks to remove the layer of sticky mucilage before being laid out to dry. This washing process removes some of the sugars and bitterness so the coffee should have a higher acidity and lighter body.

Hannah Davies

'A COFFEE WITH 90 OR MORE POINTS WILL USUALLY BE QUITE EXCLUSIVE, TASTY AND EXPENSIVE!'

INDEX

Entry no

	Entry no
108 Coffee House	122
Almond Thief, The	62
Amid Giants & Idols	53
Annie and the Flint	109
Antler and Bird	145
Artigiano - Cardiff	82
Artigiano - Exeter	115
Bakers and Co	86
Bakesmiths	21
Bath Coffee Company, The	38
Bayards Cove Inn	64
Bearpit Social	29
Beatroot Cafe	93
Beatsworkin	61
Bike Shed Cafe	111
Boscanova	48
Boston Tea Party - Barnstaple	110
Boston Tea Party - Bath	32
Boston Tea Party - Cheltenham	12
Boston Tea Party - Exeter	113
Boston Tea Party - Honiton	108
Boston Tea Party - Park Street	92
Boston Tea Party - Plymouth	66
Brazier Coffee Roasters	137
Brew & Bake	14
Brew Coffee Company	22
Bristol Coffee House	88
Bristolian Cafe, The	89
Brodies Coffee Co	80
Cafe at 36	118
Cafe Ronak	87
Calm Coffee Bar	44
Calypso Coffee Company	63
Cascara	34
Chandos Deli - Bath	100
Chandos Deli - Bristol	85
Chandos Deli - Exeter	116
Charlie Fridays Coffee Shop	58
City Deli	96
Clifton Coffee Roasters	131
Coaltown Coffee Roasters	127

	Entry no
Coasters Coffee Company	65
Coffee Dispensary, The	13
Coffee Factory	138
Coffee Gondola, The	16
Coffee Lab UK	104
Coffee Punks	4
Coffee Saloon	50
Coffi Bank	79
Colonna & Small's	37
Cotswold Artisan Coffee	75
Crankhouse Coffee	140
Crediton Coffee Company	112
Dancing Goat, The	106
Devon Coffee	114
Dusty Ape	133
Early Bird, The	78
Espressini	123
Espresso Kitchen	49
Este Kitchen	17
EXE Coffee Roasters	149
EXE Coffee Roasters - cafe	117
Exploding Bakery	56
Extract Coffee Roasters	130
Finca - Dorchester	51
Finca - Yeovil	45
Footprint Coffee	125
Forum Coffee House, The	103
Friska - Queen's Road	91
Friska - Victoria Street	97
Full Court Press	95
Ginhaus Deli	2
Glorious Art House, The	55
Good Vibes Cafe	69
Green Bird Cafe, The	99
Green Rocket Cafe	102
Greengages Coffee House and Restaurant	47
Gylly Beach Cafe	71
Hub St Ives	72
Hunter & Sons	101
Ivan's Coffee	57
Jacka Bakery	119

	Entry no		Entry no
Jacob's Coffee House	36	Small Street Espresso	28
James Gourmet Coffee Co	126	Society Cafe - High Street	35
Just Ground Coffee Kiosk	26	Society Cafe - Kingsmead Square	39
KIN+ILK - Cathedral Road	81	Soulshine	52
KIN+ILK - Tyndall Street	10	South Coast Roast - cafe	105
Lew's Coffee Shop	5	South Coast Roast Coffee Roasters	135
Leykers Coffee Central	46	Spicer+Cole - Clifton	90
Liberty Coffee	67	Spicer+Cole - Gloucester Road	18
Little and Long Coffee Roasters	146	Spicer+Cole - Queen Square	98
Little Man Coffee Company, The	9	Square Peg Coffee House	3
Little Victories	24	Square Root Coffee	134
Littlestone Coffee	150	Star Anise Arts Cafe	15
Love From Marjorie	59	Strangers with Coffee	42
Lufkin Coffee Roasters	128	Strong Adolfos	68
Lufkin Coffee Roasters - cafe	6	Tincan Coffee Co.	30
Mockingbird	20	Tincan Coffee Co. Trucks	31
Mokoko - Bath	40	Tradewind Espresso	19
Mokoko - Bristol	25	Two Day Coffee Roasters	147
New England Coffee House	11	Uncommon Ground Coffee Roastery	8
No12 Easton	94	Voyager Coffee Roasters	141
Number 35 Coffee House & Kitchen	107	Waterloo Tea - Penarth	84
Olfactory Coffee Roasters	143	Waterloo Tea - Penylan	77
Olive Co Cafe	120	Waterloo Tea - Wyndham	83
Origin Coffee	144	Wild Thyme Cafe	60
Origin Coffee at Harbour Head	124	Wright's Food Emporium	1
Picnic Coffee	33	Yallah Coffee	151
Picnic Cornwall	70	Yellow Canary Cafe, The	73
Pinkmans	23	Yeo Valley HQ	43
Plan Cafe, The	7		
Playground Coffee House	27		
RAVE Coffee	129		
Reads Coffee	136		
Reads Roastbox	54		
Relish Food & Drink	121		
River House, The	41		
Roasted Rituals Coffee	148		
Roastworks Coffee Co.	139		
Rookery, The	76		
Round Hill Roastery	132		
Sabins Small Batch Roasters	142		
Scandinavian Coffee Pod, The	74		

COFFEE NOTES

Somewhere to save details of specific brews and beans you've enjoyed

COFFEE
NOTES

MAPS

CITY CENTRE MAPS

Cardiff	169
Bristol	170
Bath	172
Exeter	173

SOUTH WEST AND SOUTH WALES MAP   178

Includes all entries not on a city map.

CAFES

ROASTERS

MORE GOOD CUPS

MORE GOOD ROASTERS

All locations shown are approximate.

CARDIFF

Cafes

Lufkin Coffee Roasters	6
Plan Cafe, The	7
Uncommon Ground Coffee Roastery	8
Little Man Coffee Company, The	9
KIN+ILK - Tyndall Street	10

Roasters

Lufkin Coffee Roasters	128

More good cups

Early Bird, The	78
Coffi Bank	79
Brodies Coffee Co	80
KIN+ILK - Cathedral Road	81
Artigiano	82
Waterloo Tea	83

BRISTOL

Cafes

Este Kitchen		**17**
Spicer+Cole		**18**
Tradewind Espresso		**19**
Mockingbird		**20**
Bakesmiths		**21**
Brew Coffee Company		**22**
Pinkmans		**23**
Little Victories		**24**
Mokoko		**25**
Just Ground Coffee Kiosk		**26**
Playground Coffee House		**27**
Small Street Espresso		**28**
Bearpit Social		**29**
Tincan Coffee Co.		**30**
Tincan Coffee Co. Trucks		**31**

Roasters

Extract Coffee Roasters	**130**

More good cups

Bakers and Co	**86**
Cafe Ronak	**87**
Bristol Coffee House	**88**
Bristolian Cafe, The	**89**
Spicer+Cole - Clifton	**90**
Friska - Queen Street	**91**
Boston Tea Party - Park Street	**92**
Beatroot Cafe	**93**
No12 Easton	**94**
Full Court Press	**95**
City Deli	**96**
Friska - Victoria Street	**97**
Spicer+Cole - Queen Square	**98**

More good roasters

Two Day Coffee Roasters	**147**

BATH

Cafes

Boston Tea Party		32
Picnic Coffee		33
Cascara		34
Society Cafe - High Street		35
Jacob's Coffee House		36
Colonna & Small's		37
Bath Coffee Company, The		38
Society Cafe - Kingsmead Sq		39
Mokoko		40

More good cups

Green Bird Cafe, The		99
Chandos Deli		100
Hunter & Sons		101
Green Rocket Cafe		102
Forum Coffee House, The		103

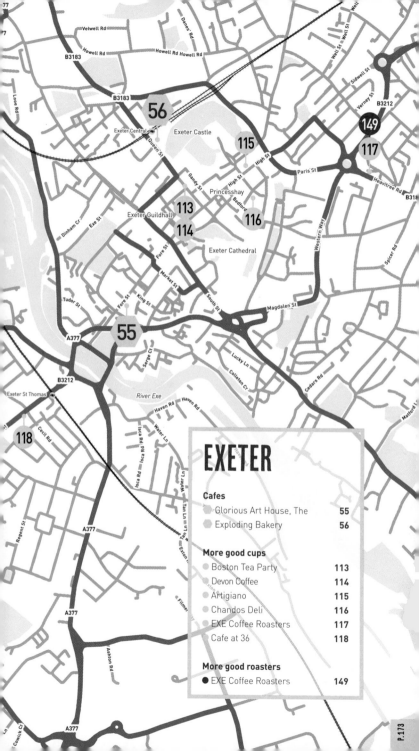

EXETER

Cafes

Glorious Art House, The   **55**
Exploding Bakery   **56**

More good cups

Boston Tea Party   **113**
Devon Coffee   **114**
Artigiano   **115**
Chandos Deli   **116**
EXE Coffee Roasters   **117**
Cafe at 36   **118**

More good roasters

EXE Coffee Roasters   **149**

ROASTERS

- Footprint Coffee — 125
- James Gourmet Coffee Co — 126
- Coaltown Coffee Roasters — 127
- Rave Coffee — 129
- Clifton Coffee Roasters — 131
- Round Hill Roastery — 132
- Dusty Ape — 133
- Square Root Coffee — 134
- South Coast Roast Coffee Roasters — 135
- Reads Coffee — 136
- Brazier Coffee Roasters — 137
- Coffee Factory — 138
- Roastworks Coffee Co. — 139
- Crankhouse Coffee — 140
- Voyager Coffee Roasters — 141
- Sabins Small Batch Roasters — 142
- Olfactory Coffee Roasters — 143
- Origin Coffee — 144
- Antler and Bird — 145

MORE GOOD CUPS

- Scandinavian Coffee Pod, The — 74
- Cotswold Artisan Coffee — 75
- Rookery, The — 76
- Waterloo Tea - Penylan — 77
- Waterloo Tea - Penarth — 84
- Chandos Deli - Bristol — 85
- Coffee Lab UK — 104
- South Coast Roast — 105
- Dancing Goat, The — 106
- Number 35 Coffee House & Kitchen — 107
- Boston Tea Party - Honiton — 108
- Annie and the Flint — 109
- Boston Tea Party - Barnstaple — 110
- Bike Shed Cafe — 111
- Crediton Coffee Company — 112
- Jacka Bakery — 119
- Olive Co Cafe — 120
- Relish Food & Drink — 121
- 108 Coffee House — 122
- Espressini — 123
- Origin Coffee at Harbour Head — 124

MORE GOOD ROASTERS

- Little and Long Coffee Roasters — 146
- Roasted Rituals Coffee — 148
- Littlestone Coffee — 150
- Yallah Coffee — 151

SOUTH WEST AND SOUTH WALES MAP

Includes all entries not on a city map.

CAFES

ROASTERS

MORE GOOD CUPS

MORE GOOD ROASTERS

CAFES

Wright's Food Emporium	1
Ginhaus Deli	2
Square Peg Coffee House	3
Coffee Punks	4
Lew's Coffee Shop	5
New England Coffee House	11
Boston Tea Party - Cheltenham	12
Coffee Dispensary, The	13
Brew & Bake	14
Star Anise Arts Cafe	15
Coffee Gondola, The	16
River House, The	41
Strangers with Coffee	42
Yeo Valley HQ	43
Calm Coffee Bar	44
Finca - Yeovil	45
Leykers Coffee Central	46
Greengages Coffee House	47
Boscanova	48
Espresso Kitchen	49
Coffee Saloon	50
Finca - Dorchester	51
Soulshine	52
Amid Giants & Idols	53
Reads Roastbox	54
Ivan's Coffee	57
Charlie Fridays Coffee Shop	58
Love From Marjorie	59
Wild Thyme Cafe	60
Beatsworkin	61
Almond Thief, The	62
Calypso Coffee Company	63
Bayards Cove Inn	64
Coasters Coffee Company	65
Boston Tea Party - Plymouth	66
Liberty Coffee	67
Strong Adolfos	68
Good Vibes Cafe	69
Picnic Cornwall	70
Gylly Beach Cafe	71
Hub St Ives	72
Yellow Canary Cafe, The	73

OPEN THE DOORS

TO A WORLD OF SPECIALITY COFFEE

SEE PAGE 169

SEE PAGE 170

SEE PAGE 172

SEE PAGE 173

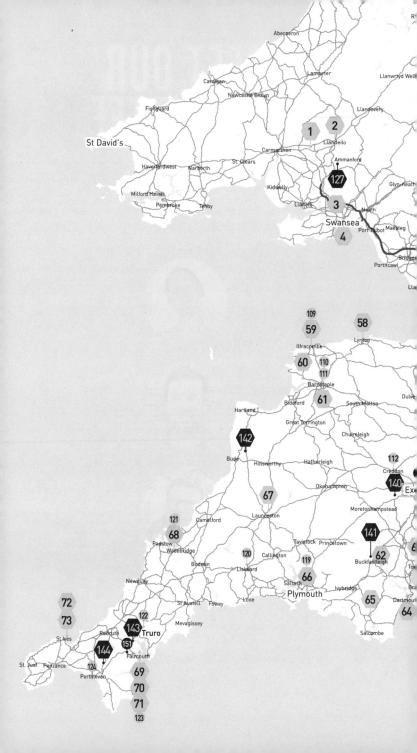

MEET OUR COMMITTEE

The South West and South Wales Independent Coffee Guide's committee is made up of a small band of coffee experts and enthusiasts who've worked with Salt Media and the coffee community to oversee this year's guide

DAISY ROLLO

ANDREW TUCKER

ED GOODING

NICK COOPER